MENNONITE LOW GERMAN PROVERBS FROM KANSAS

Low German / English / Standard German

Threshing stone, Mennonite Heritage Museum
Goessel, Kansas [author]

Isaias J. McCaffery

MENNONITE LOW GERMAN PROVERBS FROM KANSAS

Copyright © 2008 by Isaias J. McCaffery

First Edition

Mennonite Heritage Museum
Goessel, KS

Printed in the USA by Lulu.com, Morrisville, NJ

ISBN: 978-0-6152-3559-2

Photos courtesy of www.freeimages.co.uk

FORWORD

"Prof. McCaffery has laboured long and hard on this valuable contribution to Plautdietsch lore, folkways, humour, and yes, history! To readers of our beloved mother tongue of Plautdietsch, this collection will provide many hours of pleasure, reminiscence, even joy, bringing back to life concepts, ideas, and commonalities many of us have known and experienced-- but have forgotten or inadvertently left behind through circumstances and conditions. The infinitely varied sources of these proverbs will demonstrate an unexpected breadth and width.... Much of this wisdom has been filtered and become an integral part of what we accept as generally applicable expressions of truth, by which we have long attempted to live.

We owe Dr. McCaffery an enormous thank you for putting this huge collection of proverbs together. Even though he is not a "native" speaker of Plautdietsch, he has achieved a deep understanding and love of the language, and has fully demonstrated that love by the persistence and loyalty to his goal of making this collection available to the rest of us. Congratulations, Isaias! We'll enjoy!"

Eldo Neufeld, author of Plautdietsch Humour, Plautdietsch Verb Conjugation & related
                    works
Vancouver, British Columbia

CONTENTS

INTRODUCTION

When speakers of Mennonite Low German began fleeing the Russian Empire in the 1870s, most crossed the Atlantic with few material possessions. Their wooden trunks bore the hand-lettered names of the immigrants' and contained clothing, linen, photos, tea cups, Bibles, wedding and baptismal certificates, stashes of gold rubles, and small keepsakes. Many travelers also carried precious seeds for growing favorite strains of vegetables, flowers and winter wheat—the living agricultural heritage of their forefathers.

These were people whose ancestors had first fled eastward from Holland, northwest Germany, Flanders and Frisia in search of religious tolerance amid the sandy lowlands along the Baltic Sea. When the situation in the delta near the city of Danzig deteriorated, the "Dutch" Mennonites—now speaking a West Prussian dialect of Low German-- fled eastward yet again. They accepted Imperial Russia's offer of land and a right to communal self-government, and what followed was almost a century of relative harmony, growth and prosperity. But by 1870, Czar Alexander II was revoking the colonists' traditional privileges, seeking universal military service from young Mennonite men and the adoption of the Russian language in the classroom. So began the break-up of some of Russia's most productive agricultural communities—a process that Joseph Stalin completed violently a few decades later.

What this volume contains are some of the "invisible" treasures that migratory people always carry over horizons and across oceans— their traditional sayings, proverbs and rhymes that contain generations of wisdom, advice, commentary and criticism. The roots of proverbs are twisted and deep, with some stretching back to the Romans, ancient Greeks, Persians, Arabs, wandering Germanic and Slavic tribes, early Indo-European farmers and pastoral nomads—back deep into the neolithic and perhaps the paleolithic ages of prehistory. Over the centuries, inspiration came from the Bible, the barnyard, the plow, the seasons, the social order of medieval lord and serf, and out of the natural cycles of birth, life and death. Folk sayings respected no borders, but continually cross-pollinated and mutated until many now exist in dozens of variations and scores of languages. National pride of ownership is commonplace, while concrete proof of origins is often elusive.

My goal has been to help preserve a cultural heritage that enriches my home state of Kansas, encourage the study, use and preservation of an interesting but endangered dialect, and to experience considerable enjoyment in the process. The last item is a given…

Isaias J. McCaffery

Independence Community College, Independence, KS

PLAUTDIETSCH PRONUNCIATION

The following tables will facilitate an understandable pronunciation, but the *best* way to learn is by listening to native speakers and imitating them. Keep in mind that dialects *vary* among Plautdietsch (PD) speakers, although all are mutually intelligible.

PD Consonants: **b, d, f, h, k, l, m, n, p, r, t**   are about the same as in English.

c	is only used in ch and sch.
g	is hard like the sound in the English word "good."
gj	is a soft flat "g."
j	sounds like the letter "y" in "yellow."
kj	is a soft flat "k." Some Molotschna-descent speakers say "tj."
s	soft like the "z" in "zero."
sch	pronounced "sh" in "sheep."
st	pronounced "sht."
sp	pronounced "shp."
ss	hard like the "s" in "sack." Some say "ts."
w	has the sound of English "v."
zh	like the "j" in French "bonjour" or "x" in English "luxurious"

PD Vowels:

a	sounds like the "a" in "father."
ä	is a long "a" like in "fate" or a short "a" like "e" in "wet."
ää	shorter, but not a diphthong
äa	is a diphthong employing the long "ä" and "a" described above.
au	sounds like the ow in "cow" but is often shorter
e	is short as in "let."
ee	is something like the "a" in "fame."
ei	like the "i" in "mind" or "find"
i	can be short like the "i" in "bit"-- or long like the "i" in "machine."
ie	is like "ee" in "tree."
o	can be short as in "hop"--

	or long as in "rope."
oa	is something like "<u>oa</u>" in "boa" or "Samoa," flattened like "aw" in "saw" but with the two vowels still distinctly voiced.
oo	is something like "<u>oa</u>" in "boat"
u	sounds like the "u" in "put."
uu, ü	is something like the deep "u" in "mule."

* v	has an "f" sound in many Plautdietsch spelling systems, but is omitted by Herman Rempel

* d	at the *end* of a word generally sounds like a "t."

For helpful free online audio recordings with written texts, try www.biblegateway.com which offers a Plautdietsch translation of the Bible. Click on the Reimer2001 version.

HIGH GERMAN PRONUNCIATION

Here is a basic guide to High German pronunciation. Even if your main interest is Plautdietsch (PD), it may be helpful to understand the standard German spelling system because many PD speakers use it in modified forms when they write. Also, traditional Mennonite prayers are learned and recited in Hochdeutsch (HD).

HD Consonants: **b, d, f, h, l, m, n, p, r, t** *are the same as English.*

c	*appears in ch and sch, and in foreign words like "cola."*
g	*is normally hard like in the word "girl."*
j	*is like the English "y" in "yellow."*
s	*can be soft like a "z"- especially at the start of a word, or hard like in "sit."*
sch	*sounds like "sh" in "shirt."*
sp	*sounds like "shp."*
st	*sounds like "sht."*
ß	*this character, the "eszett," is pronounced like an "s."*
q	*always followed by a "u," it sounds like "kv."*
th	*sounds like the English "t."*
v	*sounds like English "f."*
w	*sounds like English "v."*
z	*pronounced like "ts."*

HD Vowels:

a	*usually sounds like "a" in "father."*
ä	*can be like "a" in "gate" or "e" in "met."*

aa	*sounds like "ai" in "hair."*
au	*like "ow" in "how" or "ou" in "mouse."*
e	*as in "bed."*
e	*at the end of a word, like "a" in "ago."*
ei, ai	*rhyme with "my" and "high."*
äu, eu	*like "oy" in "boy."*
i	*long and short values like in English.*
ie	*rhymes with "me" and "see."*
o	*long and short values like English.*
ö	*not in English; something like "ur" in "hurt."*
u	*long and short values, like the "oo" vowel in "boot." and like the "oo" vowel in "cook."*
ü	*not found in English, like the French "sur."*

PLAUTDIETSCH SPELLING

This collection includes "double" PD entries (in addition to the English and High German ones) employing two commonly used spelling systems—an older one devised by Herman Rempel, and a newer one which is the work of Reuben Epp. Many PD readers in North America still like Rempel's orthography because its use of the alphabet resembles our English forms, and Rempel's handy paperback dictionary is inexpensive and now available for use on-line. Reuben Epp, on the other hand, offers a system that is much more compatible with prevailing Low German spellings, making it accessible to a wider community of some 8 million *Plattduutsch* readers. In my [debatable] opinion, the Epp orthography is now the preferred standard. One of the most noticeable differences between the Epp and Rempel systems is that the former retains the use of the German "v", while the latter does not. Epp uses the letters "v" and "f" to represent the *same* spoken consonant in conformity with traditional German spellings. He also employs a silent "h" in certain words so that they resemble their High German cousins. While this can add a slim margin of complexity for English speakers, it is of *great* help for readers familiar with German. Both Epp and Rempel utilize infinitive verb forms that omit a final "n." While certain Old Colony-origin PD dialects have retained the "n," this difference should not compromise the reader's understanding. By including duel entries in Plautdietsch, plus English and High German, I hope to maximize comprehension, and allow readers to compare the language(s) they know with the ones they are learning. An added advantage is that differences between the duel PD versions often reflect real variations that exist within the spoken dialect.

I should make it plain that this work contains my best efforts to conform to the Rempel and Epp's orthographies, based on available guides. Reuben Epp graciously corrected and updated some early drafts by e-mail, undoubtedly resulting in a better final product. Like many serious linguists he is a committed perfectionist, and is still at work fine-tuning his spelling system-- so the last word on Plautdietsch writing forms is not yet written. Still another model for writers can be found in the dictionary and published works of Jack Thiessen, whose spelling scheme resembles the Epp system in most of its essentials. Thiessen, like many European writers, prefers "tj" to "kj." Differences in spelling arise partly from variations in pronunciation of the dialect, a complexity that students of language may find more enjoyable than problematic. Where I have only a single PD entry, the Epp and Rempel texts are identical. Any mistakes herein are solely mine, not those of Reuben Epp, Herman Rempel, or any other advisors, teachers or references!

INTRODUCTORY ESSAY

Mennonite Low German Sayings and Proverbs in Kansas: Language Erosion and Conservation of an Ethnic Heritage in the Wake of Language Extinction

One hundred and twenty-five years ago, Kansas was home to a remarkably diverse assortment of German dialects, each representing a unique population with its own religious traditions, songs, folklore, dress, customs, cuisine, migration experience, and distinct sense of identity or people-hood. Amounting to about forty percent of the state's population, the German-speakers remained fractured by differences of religion, speech and culture, never coalescing to wield the sort of organized influence that their numbers might imply. Hanoverians, Saxons, Rheinlanders, Württembergers, Prussians, and Bavarians all formed distinct enclaves and community networks, joined by dialect-speakers from Austria, Switzerland, Alsace and Luxembourg. In addition to these Central Europeans came transplanted Germans from Missouri, Illinois, Ohio, Wisconsin, Iowa, and Indiana, as well as substantial numbers of Pennsylvania Germans who brought their "Pennsylvania Dutch" or *Deitsch* idiom to new homes on the plains. Eastern Europe contributed thousands of dialect-speakers from Bohemia, Moravia, Bucovina (Slovakia), Hungary, Poland, Volhynia (N. Ukraine), the Ukraine, the Russian Volga region, the Crimea and beyond.

Amid this mingling of peoples in Kansas, one could find Swiss migrants direct from central Switzerland confronted by peoples of remote Swiss ancestry-- whose modified speech, food and costumes would have bewildered the Bernese settlers who had traded the Alps for the prairie. Austrians from Salzburgerland and the Tyrol and Swabians from South Germany could also encounter strange fur-capped high-booted immigrants claiming kinship to them in virtually incomprehensible dialects. A Saxon from Leipzig would have felt little in common with Saxon-descendants isolated for centuries in the medieval German enclaves of eastern Hungary-- men and women whose speech began diverging from that of other Saxons when Viking long-ships still raided Baltic fishing towns.

I like to think that if some linguistic mad-scientist had plotted to make Kansas a menagerie of German varieties, he or she could scarcely have assembled a more varied and complex mix of communities. KU Germanics Professor William Keel identifies Volga German *Deitsch*, Hannoverian *Plattdüütsch*, Swiss Volhynian *Schweitzerdeitsch*, Swiss German *Bäärntüütsch*, Bavarian Russian *Deitsch-Behmisch*, German-Russian Mennonite *Plautdietsch*, Bucovina Swabian *Schwäwisch* and Pennsylvania German *Däätsch* as just a few of the more commonly heard Kansas dialects. 1 Within each of these existed still further variations, reflecting the regional, town or village origins of the immigrants and their children, and delineating yet another degree of identity.

Having described the Babel-like conditions of more than a century ago, if one now "fast-forwards" to Kansas in the 21st century, one discovers rather bleak prospects for linguistic survival among the German-speakers. Many communities are now reduced to just a handful of extremely elderly speakers, and in many historical enclaves the dialects are completely gone. Researching the history of the Hanoverian Lutherans in southeastern Kansas, I found mere fragments of Low German among residents above seventy years of age, and not a single individual who still maintained real conversational ability. The stories, sayings, rhymes, songs and other oral traditions that these communities once possessed are now lost forever, and can only be tentatively reconstructed by examining related populations in other places. A few decades ago, an opportunity existed to preserve a least a snapshot of these people's folkloric heritage, but when that window closed it was irrevocably sealed. Although church records, census reels, plat maps and other documents can still reveal a lot about Hanoverian settlements, most of these records lack the human element of an ethnic group expressing its values, emotions and traditions in its own native speech.2

At present, central Kansas possesses one of the best opportunities in the state to conserve the oral history and traditions of a German-speaking minority. Eight years ago, while returning from a Kansas History Teachers Association (KHTA) meeting at Ft. Hays State, I was lured off the main highway by signs advertising the Mennonite Heritage Museum in Goessel and the Kaufman Museum in North Newton. During my visits I met several (live!) Low German speakers, and was invited back for a Borscht luncheon where I was promised a much larger gathering of similar folks. I was also witness to the recitation of a number of traditional *Plautdietsch* sayings and proverbs, some of which appeared to be unique to the dialect [they did not rhyme in standard German]. The very difficulty in understanding *Plautdietsch*, one of the more divergent members of the German dialect family, made it all the more enticing. People sang fragments of cradle lullabies, recounted Low German jokes, and even shared a few off-color sayings and rhymes (for which they invariably apologized). I was shown how traditional rolls (Tweeback) were cooked in a Russian-style oven fired with wheat straw, and was even sent home with samples (in case I got hungry while driving on the highway). Learning that hundreds of mostly retired *Plautdietsch* speakers still reside across a five county area, I decided to begin collecting proverbs and sayings—a task that would have been impossible without churches, museums, senior centers, assorted faculty and staff at Bethel Collge, dozens of individuals, and the power of email.3

Before going further, it would be expedient to quickly explain which Mennonite communities we are referring to, where they came from and how their Low German variant, called *Plautdietsch*, has evolved. At present, Kansas is home to about fifteen different Anabaptist church conferences or denominations, quilted together out of a complicated mix of settlers with roots stretching back five hundred years to the Reformation. 4 Of the two main ethnic branches in the Mennonite tree, the Swiss/South German and the Dutch/Frisian/Flemish/North German, the Plautdietsch-speakers belong to the latter and may be simply called Dutch Mennonites [although German, Flemish and even some Polish ancestry is also present].5 During the sixteenth century, their ancestors suffered extreme persecution in the Low Countries, where between 1500 and 2500 died gruesome deaths for their beliefs. Among their most noteworthy doctrines were the rejection of war and violence, oath-taking, infant baptism, and secular governmental power over matters of faith. The early Mennonites felt that merely to exchange a Catholic state-church for a Protestant one did little to actually reform corrupted European society, which needed a spiritual transformation based on the teachings and behavioral models found in the scripture. But with the Ottoman Turkish Muslim armies knocking at the gates of Vienna, the refusal of Anabaptist Christians to take up arms, even in self-defense, seemed like treason to some members of mainstream society.6

Fleeing death by fire and beheading, Menno Simons and many of his followers spilled eastward into German lands, settling in Schleswig-Holstein, near the cities of Hamburg and Lübeck, and within the Vistula or Weichsel River delta near the city of Danzig. For nearly two centuries, the Dutch Mennonites flourished in West Prussia, and here they adopted and modified the local Low German dialect as the language of home. At church, the Dutch language was stubbornly maintained until the mid-1700s, and later surviving Dutch Bibles made the journey to Kansas in the 1870s.7 After initial epidemics of malaria ceased, the people prospered on the Baltic coast, and in addition to farming they labored in nearly every occupation, including work as merchants, bankers, millers, doctors and skilled craftsmen. Eventually, this idyllic existence along the Vistula River was threatened, when in the 1870's steep new taxes were demanded to purchase continued exemption from military service. The Prussian state also enacted new laws prohibiting of sale of additional land to the Mennonites, forcing many of the young to become landless tenants. Additional taxes were also collected to support the Lutheran state-church, whose practices violated many Mennonite principles. In short, the Prussian government was showing less and less tolerance toward the two-hundred year-old Dutch Mennonite community residing on its territory.8

For many Mennonites along the Baltic, conditions called for yet another wrenching migration. This time the recruitment efforts of the Russian Empire, which promised generous land grants, the right for colonies to create their own local governments and schools, and the critical exemption from military service proved quite effective. The first

Ukrainian settlement, located along a tributary of the Dnieper River, was the Chortitza or "Old Colony" founded in 1789. An area approximately 20x30 miles was granted for the Mennonites to develop, but within this region were scattered Ukrainian villages as well. A few years later in 1804, a second settlement was begun along the Molotschnaya River 75 miles to the southeast. It was this milk-colored stream that lent its name to the Molotschna Colony. The largest Mennonite colony ever established in Russia, the Molotschna villages were spread over a 25x40 mile area. Migration from German to Russian lands continued until the 1830s, and ultimately over 70 distinct Mennonite villages existed within Chortitza and Molotschna, with daughter colonies spreading south to the Crimean Peninsula and eventually to the Caucasus and parts of Central Asia.9

After nearly a century on Russian soil, conditions began to deteriorate as they had earlier in Prussia. The government of Czar Alexander II lost tolerance for the ethnic separatism of the Mennonites, and began revoking many of the privileges that had attracted them in the first place. Now school was to be conducted in the Russian language, and young men were to perform their military service. Eventually an option for alternative service in forestry was created, in a belated effort to stem immigration, but for many Mennonites the new policy of "Slavification" was unacceptable. The people were told that they were to acquire and adopt the Russian language within ten years, or presumably lose everything they had built in Russia. Meanwhile, further expansion of Mennonite land holdings was prohibited, and by 1870, with a growing population, two-thirds of the forty-five thousand colonists had no land at all.10

By 1873, a delegation of Mennonite elders was touring central Kansas, earnestly in search of good farm land for settlement. Instrumental in bringing the Russian

15

Mennonites to the state was an agent of the Santa Fe Railroad, Carl Bernhard Schmidt, who was born in Prussian-controlled Saxony and spoke both High and Low German. Schmidt later crossed the Atlantic and toured the southern Ukraine as an immigration recruiter, armed with the letters of successfully transplanted Kansas Mennonites (a venture that the Russian authorities abruptly terminated). Some 800 immigrants from the Molotschna village of Alexanderwohl, led by elders Jacob Buller and Dietrich Gaeddert, arrived the following year, purchasing large tracts of railroad land at $2.50 an acre—half the going rate at the time. The Santa Fe also built temporary housing for the immigrants, provided free passenger passes from the East Coast, and delivered the settlers' wooden chests, wagons, and other bulky luggage free of charge. In addition to the Russian Mennonites, smaller contingents of Prussian and Swiss Volhynian Mennonites also established nearby communities in the early 1870s, beginning a steady flow of immigration that would continue into the 1920s.11

Plautdietsch dialects were spoken by a number of distinct populations settling in Marion, Reno, Harvey, McPherson and northwest Butler counties. The largest number came from villages affiliated with the Molotschna Colony, but substantial numbers of "Old Colony" or Chortitza immigrants also took up residence in the area. Several congregations of West Prussians, Mennonites who had skipped the century-long sojourn into Russia, also arrived and built churches at Brudertal, Newton and Whitewater. Enclaves of Crimean Mennonites, speaking their own Plautdietsch variants, were also organized at Gnadenau, Inman and Lehigh.12

Yet another Low German-speaking group were the Dutch (or Prussian) Volhynian Poles, who had settled for 75 years near the Polish city of Ostrog, in the villages of

Grüntal, Karlswalde and Karlsberg. They arrived speaking a dialect that could scarcely be understood by the South Russians, and were further marginalized by their relative poverty and limited farming skills. Residing as tenants on the wilderness estates of wealthy Polish lords, these Mennonites took up forestry work that was later ill-suited to life in Central Kansas. Organized congregations of these Ostrogers were located at Canton, Lehigh and Pawnee Rock. A related group of Low German speakers were families of Dutch Poles from further south, who originated from daughter colonies such as Michalin, Antanofka, and Waldheim. These immigrants crossed the Atlantic independently to establish their own communities near Hillsboro and Whitewater. So impoverished were the Dutch Polish Mennonites that initially they required considerable charity just to survive, and received the label of "the Helpless Poles" from neighboring Mennonite communities.13

With such a varied mix of peoples, the heirs of such a tangled history of repeated migrations, understandable confusion existed as to how to categorize both the settlers and their language. Were these people to be considered Dutchmen, Prussians, Russians or Poles? Was their language a type of modified Dutch or an odd variety of German? Was Low German an inferior, corrupted patois that was "low down," as its name seemed to suggest? Both native-born Americans and the Mennonites themselves argued over these questions, and the literature today expresses various points of view.

Distinctions of "low" versus "high" refer to altitude rather than quality, with the various dialects of *Plattdeutsch* being native to the lowlands of the Northern European coast. The word "platt" is a cognate of the English "flat," an apt description of the North German Plain. In its heyday, Low German enjoyed great prestige during the late Middle

Ages when the North German Hanseatic League dominated Baltic and North Sea trade, and today modern Scandinavian languages like Danish and Swedish still bear the strong imprint of Low German. With the collapse of the Hansa, and Martin Luther's decision in 1522 to translate his Bible into a Middle German idiom, the national linguistic standard of the Germans shifted southward.14

When compared with other Germanic languages, it becomes clear that Mennonite *Plautdietsch* belongs to the Lower Prussian subgroup of the greater family of Low German dialects that once stretched from the Netherlands to Lithuania. It is a linear descendant of Middle and Old Saxon, and can thus be connected to writings dating back to at least the ninth century. In the words of one linguist, *Plautdietsch* "should probably be called Low Saxon rather than Low German, to clarify the fact that it is not a dialect of High German." 15 Low German missed a series of critical sound shifts that altered the pronunciation of High German during the seventh and ninth centuries, and thus it shares a number of features exhibited by English--which was brought to the British Isles by Germanic tribes before the changes occurred on the mainland. This explains the striking similarity between Low German words like *Aupel, deep, Drepp, Foot, Tung, Water,* and their English equivalents. *Plautdietsch* in Kansas might best be described as aWest Prussian dialect with some Dutch, Flemish and Frisian flourishes, an admixture of Russian and Ukrainian vocabulary, and a final dose of English loan-words— used mainly to describe technological inventions such as automobiles, radios, telephones, and cornflakes that arrived on the scene after immigration to America.16

While collecting Low German sayings, an obvious historical question presented itself, posed by the distinct demographic profile of my sources. Not a single Low German speaker among the dozens with whom I spoke appeared to be younger than the age of sixty, and the majority were clearly in their seventies and eighties. Two noteworthy exceptions turned out to be younger persons who had moved to Kansas from Canada and Paraguay, where they had learned the dialect as children. Clearly something had occurred during the 1940s and '50's, which resulted in the so-called baby-boomers not acquiring Plautdietsch within their childhood homes. Eldo Neufeld, a Canadian Low German expert who was raised in Inman, Kansas, confirmed that within his own extended family, peer group, and community, the forties and fifties were "the critical years" of language loss. Now the task was to determine what factors had triggered the break in language transmission that put the dialect on the path to extinction in central Kansas.17 *Plautdietsch* had flourished in the United States for eighty years before a critical mid-twentieth century cohort of parents and children failed to exchange this part of their ethnic heritage—and unlike many cases of language decline, the "transmission failure" seems to have been fairly abrupt and nearly universal.

As David Engbrecht explains in his study of the Americanization of General Conference Mennonites in Kansas, the process of language transition was twofold. In church the people changed from High German to English, while at home and in daily conversation the move was from *Plautdietsch* to English. In the case of most Dutch Mennonites after 1900, it was the clergy and conference leadership that were pushing to complete the "inevitable" transition to English, advocating change in advance of the inclination of many congregations. Given the differing attitudes among Polish Russians, Dutch Volhynians, Dutch Prussians and South Russian congregations, the actual arrival of English sermons in local churches varied from as early as 1900 to as late as the 1940s.

Engbrecht cites the exposure of the Dutch Mennonites to more Americanized Mennonites from the eastern United States as an important factor in speeding the transition to English. However, he admits that the transition of language in the churches did not directly coincide with the abandonment of dialect-use in everyday life. For example, in the town of Goessel, *Plautdietsch* remained the everyday mode of communication for at least ten years after High German had yielded to English in the pulpit.[18] Still, it is safe to assume that the adoption of English in church to some extent facilitated and offered justification for the abandonment of Low German in the home. Given the central role of churches in Mennonite society, the example set by pastors and elders would surely have influenced the thinking of many community members.

Another commonly cited explanation for the erosion of German language-use was the trauma of anti-German hysteria of the First World War, followed by the added stigma of Nazism on all things German during and after World War II. James Juhnke chronicles the hardships endured by Kansas Mennonites during the Great War, in which state law banned the use of the German language, while vigilantes harassed and abused Mennonite "slackers" who declined to purchase war bonds. Young conscientious objectors received military hazings that included beatings with fists and rubber hoses, death threats, bread-and-water diets, ritual humiliations and long stretches in solitary confinement. Meanwhile arsonists burned Tabor College's main building to the ground, while in some localities patriotic deputies confiscated families' German Bibles.[19] As bad as the experience of WWI was for Kansas Mennonites, it was hardly a mortal blow to the vitality of Low German. Instead, the World Wars added to the social discomfort of being part of an ethnic minority, and undoubtedly played a role in some families' decision to embrace English. On the other hand, many Mennonites accepted periodic persecution as part of their historic identity, and thousands of Anabaptists in North America continue to propagate their own German dialects regardless of the legacy of war.

The World Wars affected Low German-speaking Mennonites in other ways besides their exposure to Anglo-American hostility and xenophobia. Anecdotal evidence suggests that (relatively) high-paying war-time jobs in Wichita, Kansas City and other urban areas lured many young people away from the depression-era farms and small towns of their youth, severing ethnic ties and requiring the daily use of English. Once they left home, many of these young people never returned, accept for the occasional holiday visit. Carol Coburn's work on German Lutherans and Carl F. Bowman's study the Church of the Brethren both document a similar cultural "shearing effect" connected with the world wars.20

Another impact of the Second World War, now a painful subject for some Dutch Mennonites to recall, was the military service performed by many of their men. Alternative service was available for conscientious objectors in Civilian Public Service camps, but far fewer Dutch Mennonites adhered to their churches anti-war traditions than had in 1917. Since the 1940s, the community rejection of war has rebounded , but during World War II hundreds of Kansas Mennonite youth put on uniforms, and at least ten of them: Edward Buller, John Boese, Pete Boese, Abe Ensz, Irwin Harder, Jonathan Jantz, Herbert Janzen, William Klassen, Dietrich Rempel and Leo Warkentin were killed in action serving in the U.S. Army and Army Air Corps. Given the typical ratio of killed to wounded during the war, it is likely that over 500 Mennonites from Marion, Harvey, Reno and McPherson counties served as combatants overseas, with significant consequences for their ethnic and religious identities.21 Even those who performed

alternative service as conscientious objectors were transported far from home, and

exposed to the influences fellow pacifists from a variety of backgrounds, including

people who were sometimes eager to convert rural Mennonite farm boys to their own

religions.22

In attempting to understand language loss among the baby-boomers, I decided upon a

strategy not employed in by most published sources, which was to simply ask living

Kansas Mennonites what happened, based upon their own experiences. Then, when

possible, I attempted to substantiate their ideas with more traditional evidence. A

recurrent theme that surfaced when my sources recalled the forties and fifties was the

effect of exogamy, or "marrying outside" the ethnic community. One of the best

comments that I received was the following one from Eldo Neufeld:

> "I'd say well over half of Inman residents and [the] surrounding area of
> my generation [1950s] married out. I remember thinking, gee, he's
> marrying a girl from Inman!.... I have never had, and do not now have, the
> impression that this marrying out was a way of escaping. Going to
> College was a way of escaping, with in many cases, predictable results.
> When I think back to the girls in my high school class, plus one or two
> years before and after, there is only one whom I ever dated, and I would
> not have wanted to be married to her....My thinking was always about
> further education, travel, etc. I saw the way through widening my limited
> and limiting horizon, in whatever method necessary. A psychiatrist might
> come to a different conclusion." [This scholarly gentlemen attended
> Bethel College, and married a Swiss Mennonite]23

If this and similar accounts are accurate, they could explain a lot about the decline of

Plautdietsch in Central Kansas. With more and more households lacking everyday

parental conversation in Low German, there would be much less opportunity for children to pick up the language. Bilingual Dutch Mennonite spouses likely switched to English, given the difficulty that their partners would experience in acquiring Low German with no dictionaries, grammars or formal instruction available. The very fact that these Mennonites chose to "marry out" might also indicate less attachment to their ethnic heritage. A 1940 master's thesis by Otto D. Unruh reported that "If a Mennonite marries outside of the fold the occasion is talked of, frowned upon, and watched with a great deal of criticism." Unruh observed that during his data collection period in the late 1930s "intermarriage with non-Mennonites very seldom" occurred, and when it did, it often involved the young person leaving the church.24

I decided to test the premise of growing exogamy by examining country marriage records. I chose to examine documents from Marion County, given the fact that it covers a large geographic area of dense Mennonite settlement, rivaled only by neighboring McPherson County. The results showed that as early as 1930, 21% of Dutch / Russian Mennonites were already marrying out, although half of the non-Mennonite spouses in these cases were still ethnic Germans. One ceremony occurred in a private house, and another couple went to Abilene to say their vows before a probate judge. Given the stigma associated with choosing a spouse from outside the community, these weddings were probably transacted quietly, which may explain why Unruh used the term "seldom." A decade later, the rate of exogamy had tripled to 64%, with mixed couples arranging ceremonies in Baptist, Christian, Presbyterian, and Lutheran churches. Four couples opted for a civil ceremony, and one was married in a Volhynian Swiss Mennonite Church in Moundridge. Eight mixed weddings also occurred in Dutch Mennonite Churches, suggesting growing acceptance of the practice.25

This data bears witness to a major change taking place with a clear bearing on language erosion, but it is not sufficient to declare the "case closed." Data for 1950 unexpectedly showed a dramatic rise back up to 61% endogamous marriages, although this data may be skewed, given the fact that nearly half the cases of Dutch Mennonite marrying fellow Dutch Mennonite occurred within a single church—the Alexanderwohl congregation near Goessel. Several published sources as well as anecdotal evidence identifies Goessel as an especially traditional community, that held onto Low German longer than most surrounding towns. Several additional endogamous marriages involved Mennonite Brethren couples, who may also have been more traditional than many of their General Conference neighbors. Another distorting factor is the likelihood that in the more mobile world of 1950, more mixed couples chose to marry outside of Central Kansas and rates of exogamy may therefore be underrepresented in the Marion County data. In 1930, just 10% of the people getting married came from states and communities beyond the Dutch Mennonite settlement area. By 1950, the number of non-locals climbs to 33%, suggesting an obvious decline in geographic isolation. 26

The issue of change in the farm economy was another frequently cited factor in explaining cultural assimilation and language loss. Several people noted the pressure for younger sons to leave agriculture behind due to a lack of enough land to support them. Eldo Neufeld also noted that the sons of many successful Kansas farmers that he grew up with "disdained farming and became professionals of various kinds." 27 This theme of young men desiring to escape from life on the farm appears often in Mennonite literature, and is central to Low German writer Arnold Dyck's novel "Verloren in der Steppe [Lost in the Steppes]." The main character, Hans, is both attracted and repelled by rural life in his home village, but by leaving the farm he becomes a rootless and haunted person who is never really at home anywhere.28 Many urbanized Mennonites today express feelings of alienation and loss when they reflect upon being severed from their rural roots.

Just as in the case of county marriage data, U.S. census of agriculture statistics for McPherson, Marion, Reno, Harvey and Butler Counties between 1935 and 1992 confirm the changes in land-use patterns observed by residents. Over a sixty year span, the absolute number of farms in central Kansas declined by over half, while the size of remaining farms rose steadily as economic viability demanded larger operations with greater capital investment. With the limited number of farmsteads already a problem in 1930, we can imagine that decades of land consolidation drove many young Dutch Mennonites off the farm, even as many of their peers were leaving by choice. The number of farms containing more than 1000 acres increased dramatically across the region, and in Marion County the number rose from 23 to 150— or seven times the original number. In Reno, Harvey, and McPherson counties the increase was closer to a factor of ten times. In departing rural life, young people where generally leaving behind the Low German-speaking environments of childhood, and in the minds of many *Plautdietsch* and farming went together.29

The perceived inferior status of Low German again and again surfaces as a crucial factor in its decline, not just in Kansas, but in Canada, Germany and elsewhere. This closely parallels the situation that the Frisian tongue finds itself in as a minority language in northern Holland, where many regard the 2000 year-old West Germanic tongue as mere "farmer's talk." Pastor Willmar Harder of Hoffnungsau Mennonite Church did an perceptive job in explaining these negative attitudes. Harder observed that:

"There is often a stigma that Low German dialects are crude, low class, and spoken amongst the uneducated (probably from the fact that Mennonite Low German was not a written language with a body of cultural work). High German was used in Church and education and Low German was the everyday spoken language. You still hear comments about it being an "earthy language, fit for the barnyard." The 1940s-50's was a time of upward mobility for Mennonites as [the] WWII generation came back from alternative service (having seen the "world") and started building institutions such as higher education. They had seen and experienced the world and the stigma of speaking a "corrupted form of German" (again a misnomer often expressed by people about *Plautdietsch*), [that] did not help upward mobility (and also progressivism). It was not seen as noble, and those that retained it were looked down upon. Mennonite Low German suffered from a lack of self esteem…."30

Another telling anecdote was offered by Darlene Schroeder, a baby-boomer from

Goessel:

"When we went to Newton to shop, people there talked English. It was almost embarrassing to hear mom and dad talk Low German to each other. I vividly remember when my father was in the hospital before he died. He talked Low German and I talked English to him because I didn't feel fluent enough to talk Low German, though I felt awkward visiting that way and wished then that I knew more Low German. Even though my husband talks Low German, our daughters never learned to speak it. I wished they would have learned, but where would they use it?31

Many parents, like those of Pastor Clarence Rempel of Newton, made a conscious

decision not to pass the language on to their children. Given the harrowing experiences

of older German-speaking sisters who entered grade school without speaking English,

Rempel's mother and father decided to "make it easier on the boys." The family used

Low German until he was in kindergarten, and then deliberately switched to English.32

As Pastor Harder explains, concerns over "appearances" still tend to keep the use of

Plautdietsch in private and covert realms. He states that "In my home town [Inman] the

WWII generation will readily speak Low German *in private*, but will be much more reticent or even refuse to speak it publicly." 33 Stopping to buy fuel at a small town gas station in central Kansas, I personally encountered a group of older male coffee-drinkers chatting away in the dialect. When I approached to pay at the register, the volume of their voices became nearly inaudible, but then resumed its former level as I retreated to my car. I was told in passing while visiting the Goessel Senior Center that as very elderly local residents enter hospitals and nursing home and near the end of their lives, many actually speak more and more of their mother tongue and lose their English, creating the sad bilingual situations described by Darlene Schroeder. Some of the last Plautdietsch speakers in Kansas may say goodbye to loved ones across an impassible linguistic gulf [but love may be expressed without words].

Contrary to the detractors of the dialect, my exploration of Mennonite Low German has shown the dialect to be a rich, expressive, speech full of wit, irony, and creativity. Low German sayings and proverbs offer a direct channel into the collective lore, wisdom and life experiences of generations, and represent some the invisible treasures that crossed the Atlantic in addition to the immigrants' keepsakes and sacks of turkey red wheat. The dialect is full of colorful idioms such as the following: an "air-head" is a "Blaichkopp" (lead-head); a person without a backbone is a "Weekjbroot" (soft bread), squeamish people "eat with long teeth" or "Dee äte met lanje Täne." Many proverbs were recited to instill traditional Mennonite values, warn of life's hazards, and point out the frailties of human nature. Within Plautdietsch speaking populations, there is finally a growing recognition of the value contained in oral tradition, and more and more of it is being committed to paper. The irony is that it is often the best educated people who perceive the importance of what is slipping away. Canadian writer Victor Carl Friesen has collected scores of nursery rhymes, sayings and traditional expressions, while Doreen Helen Klassen has documented hundreds of pages worth of Mennonite Low German songs-- complete with musical scoring. When Klassen first started her project, many skeptics warned her that there was nothing worth collecting—again a manifestation of low cultural self-esteem.   In Germany, a high-quality magazine is now published in Detmold, complete with news, literary articles, poems, jokes, and recipes—all in idiomatic and readable Plautdietsch. Excellent translations of the Bible, expanded dictionaries, grammars, and even novels are appearing to help keep the language vibrant. Radio stations in several countries now broadcast in Low German, and the governments in Canada and Germany actively support minority languages, dialects and associated cultural activities. Internet venues have exploded in number in the past few years, despite continued debates over various spelling systems. One of the best websites, radio broadcaster Victor Sawatzky's "Opp Plautdietsch," contains an excellent trove of poems and other materials.   In central Kansas, Bethel College hosts an annual Low German play and program, and borscht suppers, tea parties and other social activities occur on a frequent basis at churches and other community venues. Inquiries into Low German classes are a common occurrence, although finding qualified and willing teachers can be a problem. Kansas has also received a recent influx of Low German speaking people from Northern Mexican colonies, who are estimated to number between three and five thousand. These new settlements are concentrated in the southwest near towns like Montezuma and in central Kansas near Whitewater. Such immigrants represent a new lease on life for the dialect, and a chance for present-day Kansans to show a greater appreciation for our state's cultural richness than was the norm during the last century.

NOTES

1. Keel, William D. "The German Heritage of Kansas: An Introduction." <u>Heritage of the Great Plains</u>, vol. 27, Summer 1994, 6-7. For a look at pioneer conditions from a sociological perspective, I like Sharon Hartin Iorio's <u>Faith's Harvest: Mennonite Identity in Northwest Oklahoma</u> (Norman: University of Oklahoma Press, 1999).

2. McCaffery, Isaias J. "Intermarriage among Hanoverian German Lutherans of Independence, Kansas- 1870-1950," KHTA Annual Meeting, FHSU, 2002; Also see Coburn, Carol K. <u>Life at Four Corners: Religion, Gender and Education in a German Lutheran Community, 1868-1945</u> (Lawrence: University Press of Kansas, 1992), p. 151.

3. Keel, William D. "From the Netherlands to Kansas: Mennonite Low German." <u>Heritage of the Great Plains</u>, vol. 27, Summer 1994, 47.

4. Hostetter, C. Nelson. <u>Anabaptist Mennonites Nationwide</u> USA (Morgentown, PA: Masthof Press, 1997), pp. 36-37.

5. Redekop, Calvin. <u>Mennonite Society</u> (Baltimore: John Hopkins University Press, 1989), 34.

6. Huebert, Helmut J. <u>Hierschau: An Example of Russian Mennonite</u> Life (Winnipeg: Springfield Publishers, 1986), 8-9.

7. Toews, J.A. <u>A History of the Mennonite Brethren Church</u> (Fresno, CA: Board of Christian Literature, 1982), 13-14.

8. Huebert, 14.

9. Toews, 15; 18.

10. Friesen, Victor Carl. <u>The Windmill Turning: Nursery Rhymes, Maxim, and Other Expressions of Western Canadian Mennonites</u> (Edmonton: University of Alberta Press, 1988), 11. Many of the items in Friesen's Canadian publication may be replicated somewhere in the unwritten folklore of Kansas, but I simply haven't encountered them. The most common expressions in his collection are repeated in mine, sometimes in a different version.

11. Jantzen, Marjorie. <u>In Earlier Days: A History of Goessel, Kansas</u> (Goessel, KS: Mennonite Immigrant Historical Foundation, 1987), 10-11. Also see Saul, Norman E. "The Migration of the Russian-Germans to Kansas," Kansas Historical Quarterly (Spring 1974, vol. 40, no. 1) for a general treatment of the immigration of Mennonites and other German-speaking groups.

12. Engbrecht, Dennis D. <u>The Americanizing of a Rural Immigrant Church</u> (New York: Garland, 1990), 52-53.

13. Unruh, Abe J. <u>The Helpless Poles</u> (Freeman, SD: Pine Hill Press, 1991), 7; 52-53; 61.

14. Barbour, Steven and Patrick Stephenson. <u>Variations in German</u> (New York: Cambridge University Press, 1990), 46-47.

15. Neufeld, Eldo. <u>Plautdietsch Grammar</u> (Munich: Lincom Europa, 2000), iii.

16. Thiessen, Jack. Mennonite Low German Dictionary (Madison, WI: Max Kade Institute, 2003), x-xii.

17. Neufeld, Eldo. Letter of Jan. 25, 2006.

18. Engbrecht, Dennis D. <u>The Americanization of a Rural Immigrant Church: The General Conference Mennonites in Central Kansas, 1874-1939</u>. (New York: Garland Publishing, 1990), pp. 80-81.

19. Juhnke, James C. <u>Vision, Doctrine, War</u> (Scottdale, PA: Herald Press, 1989), pp.218-219; 235-36.

20. Conversation with Darlene Schroeder, Director, Mennonite Heritage Museum, 03-22-2006; also see Coburn, <u>Life at Four Corners</u>, p. 151 for similar wartime experiences of German Lutherans in eastern Kansas, who took jobs away from home. Sharon Hartin Iorio's book, mentioned above, also contains good testimony of Mennonite experiences in both world wars.

21. U.S. Army and Air Corps casualty statistics for WWII for Marion, McPherson, Harvey, and Reno Counties online.

22. Juhnke, <u>Vision</u>, 237-38; John A. Hostetler also explains how service as conscientious objectors disrupted the culture of Amish young men. Hostetler, John A. <u>Amish Society</u> (Baltimore: John Hopkins University Press, 1993), p.274.

23. Eldo Neufeld letter, Jan. 27, 2006.

24. Unruh, Otto D. "Schisms of the Russian Mennonites of Harvey, McPherson and Reno Counties, Kansas," Masters Thesis, The University of Kansas, 1940, p. 108; 149.

25. Marion County Kansas Marriage License Records, Marion County District Court Offices, 1930, 1940.

26. Ibid., 1950.

27. Eldo Neufeld letter, Jan. 29, 2006.

28. Dyck, Arnold. Collected Works: Arnold Dyck Werke. Victor G. Doercksen and Harry Loewen eds. (Steinbach, Manitoba: Derksen Printers, 1985), pp. 387-390.

29. U.S. Census of Agriculture, Washington, DC: U.S. Government Printing Office, 1935, 1954, 1967, 1987, 1992.

30. Pastor Willmar Harder letter, Hoffnungsau Mennonite Church, Inman, Kansas, 02/14/2006.

31. Darlene Schroeder email, Goessel Kansas, 03/07/2006.

32. Pastor Clarence Rempel email, First Mennonite Church, Newton, Kansas, 03/06/2006.

33. Pastor Willmar Harder email, Hoffnungsau Mennonite Church, Inman, Kansas, 02/14/2006.

PLAUTDIETSCHE SPRICHWEAD
Plautdietsch Proverbs / Plattdeutsche Sprichwörter

TIET / TIME / ZEIT

1) Kjemmt Tiet, kjemmt Rot.
   Comes time, comes council.
   Kommt Zeit, kommt Rat.
   * This means "don't worry," when the time comes you'll know what to do. The right course of action or advice/council will present itself.

2) Kjemmt Sodeltiet, kjemmt Sot.
   Comes seeding time, comes seed.
   Kommt Saatzeit, kommt Saat.
   * Again, don't worry, when a major hurdle (like Spring planting) arrives, you'll have the resources you need (seeds) to cope. God will provide. These first two proverbs are often said together as a couplet.

3) Tiet es Jeld. *[Epp]*
   Tiet es Jelt. [Rempel]
   Time is money.
   Zeit ist Geld.

4) Tiet moakt de Uage op. *[Epp]*
   Tiet moakt dee Üage op. [Rempel]
   Time opens the eyes.
   Zeit öffnet die Augen.
   * With time clouded issues become clear, and illusions give way to reality. This is tied to maturity and experience. The young are sometimes foolish.

5) Tiet bringt Roose.
   Time brings roses.
   Zeit bringt Rose.
   * In time life brings rewards. If your life is presently in the gloom of winter, spring will eventually arrive. Patience is a virtue backed by faith.

6) Spoa en de Tiet, soo hast du en de Noot. *[Epp]*
   Spoa enn dee Tiet, soo hast dü enn dee Noot. [Rempel]
   Save in the [present] time, so you have in need.
   Sparen in der Zeit, so hast du in der Not.

7) Tiet wacht't fe' kjeen Maun. *[Epp]*
   Tiet wachtet fe' kjeen Maun. [Rempel]
   Time waits for no man.
   Zeit wartet für keinen Mann.

Een oole Uah. [www.freeimages.co.uk]

8) De Tiet steiht nich stell. *[Epp]*
   Dee Tiet steit nijch stell. [Rempel]
   Time does not stand still.
   Die Zeit steht nicht still.

9) Tieen Minuute ver de Tiet, es kjristliche Pinktlichkjeit. *[Epp]*
   Tian Minüte fer dee Tiet, es kjristlijche Pinkjtlijchkjeit. [Rempel]
   Ten minutes before the time, that is Christian punctuality.
   Zehn Minuten vor der Zeit, ist christliche Pünktlichkeit.
   * In Germanic societies, being on time is considered very important. This is in strong
     contrast to the casual attitude that many other nations have about punctuality.
     In many Latin countries for example, people expect and even _prefer_ a visitor to be
     late. Show up on time there, and your host may come to the door wearing pajamas.

10) Weinig un foaken moake vääl en de Tiet. *[Epp]*
   Weinijch onn foake moake fäl enn dee Tiet. [Rempel]
   Little and often makes a lot in time.
   Wenig und häufig machen viel in der Zeit.

11) Tiet deit Wundadoda. *[Epp]*
   Tiet deit Wundadoda. [Rempel]
   Time does wondrous deeds.
   Die Zeit tut Wundertaten.

12) Et nemmt weinig Tiet, vääl Goots too doone, oba uk weinig Tiet, vääl Beeset. *[Epp]*
   Et bruckt weinijch Tiet, fäl Goots too doone, oba uck weinijch Tiet, fäl Beeset. [Rempel]
   It requires little time, to do much good, but also little time to do much evil.
   Es braucht wenig Zeit, viel Gutes zu tun, aber auch wenig Zeit, viel Böses.

13) Aules ändat sikj aules met de Tiet. *[Epp]*
   Et endet sikj aules met dee Tiet. [Rempel]
   Everything changes [itself] with time.
   Es ändert sich alles mit der Zeit.

14) De Tiet moakt uk de Noare kluak. *[Epp]*
   Dee Tiet moakt uck dee Noare klüak. [Rempel]
   Time also makes fools wise.
   Die Zeit macht ach den Narren klug.

15) De Tiet lascht aules uut. *[Epp]*
   Dee Tiet lascht aules üt. [Rempel]
   Time blots everything out.
   Die Zeit löscht alles aus.

16) De Tiet woat von Dag too Dag schwanda. *[Epp]*
   Dee Tiet woat fonn Dach too Dach schwanda. [Rempel]
   The time[s] become from day to day tougher.
   Die Zeit wird von Tag zu Tag schwerer.

17) Tiet heelt aule Wunde. *[Epp]*
    Tiet heelt aule Wunde. [Rempel]
    The time heals all wounds.
    Zeit heilt alle Wunden.

18) De Tiede ändre sikj, un wi ons met ahn. *[Epp]*
    Dee Tiede endre sikj, onn wie ons met an. [Rempel]
    The times change themselves and we [change] ourselves with them.
    Die Zeiten ändern sich und wir uns mit ihnen.

19) Tiet bringt aules, fe' soone dee wachte kjenne. *[Epp]*
    Tiet bringt aules, fe' dee Lied dee wachte kjenne. [Rempel]
    Time brings everything for the people, who can wait for it.
    Zeit bringt für die Leute alles, die es warten können.

20) Jiedre Sach haft äahre Tiet. *[Epp]*
    Jiede Sach haft äahre Tiet. [Rempel]
    Every thing has its time.
    Jede Sache hat seine Zeit.
        * This parallels Ecclesiastes 3:1-8; God has perfect timing for everything in life.
          Peace comes with yielding to God's plan, and not imposing our own.

21) De easchta Dag een G<u>aust</u>,
    De äwaje Tiet 'ne L<u>aust</u>. *[Epp]*
    Dee easchta Dach een G<u>aust</u>,
    Dee äwaje Tiet 'ne L<u>aust</u>. [Rempel]
    The first day a guest,
    The left-over time a burden.
    Der erste Tag ein Gast,
    Die übrige Zeit eine Last.
        * Even the best guest can become a burden after the initial excitement of the visit
          passes. Shorter visits don't wear out the welcome.

22) Bäta eene Stund too tiedig aus eene Minuut too lot. *[Epp]*
    Bäta eene Stund too tiedijch aus eene Minüt too lot. [Rempel]
    Better an hour too early than a minute too late.
    Besser eine Stunde zu früh als eine Minute zu spät.

23) Tiet moakt Hei.
    Time makes hay.

Zeit macht Heu.
   * *With only the passage of time a new crop of hay (and other things of value) will mature.*

24) Tiet es Oaja siene Medizien. *[Epp]*
   Tiet es Oaja siene Meditsien. [Rempel]
   Time is anger's medicine.
   Zeit ist Medizin des Zornes.
   * *With time anger abates… in most cases.*

25) Bäta lot aus nie*(mols)*.
   Better late than never.
   Besser spät als nie.

ÄTE / FOOD / ESSEN

26) De Aupel fällt nich wiet vom Staum. *[Epp]*
   Dee Aupel fällt nijch wiet fomm Staum. [Rempel]
   The apple falls not far from the tree.
   Der Apfel fällt nicht weit vom Stamm.

27) Nu mott wi em suara Aupel biete. *[Epp]*
   Nü mott wie enn dän süa Aupel biete. [Rempel]
   Now we must bite into the sour apple.
   Nun wir mussen in den sauren Apfel beißen.
   * *In other words, now we must "take the plunge" and dive into something unpleasant.*

28) Uk de gooda Aupel vedoawt. *[Epp]*
   Uck dee goota Aupel fedoawt. [Rempel]
   Even the good apple spoils.
   Auch der gute Apfel verdirbt.

29) Wan de Bäa riep es, fällt se von selwst auf. *[Epp]*
   Wan dee Bäa riep es, fällt see fonn selfst auf. [Rempel]
   If the pear is ripe, it falls off by itself.
   Wenn die Birne reif ist, fällt sie von selbst ab.
   * *When the time for an action is ripe, it will occur with ease. Try to force things, and the same task can be difficult or impossible.*

30) Et jefft vääl Bäare, oba se send nich aula Kjoasche. *[Epp]*
Et jeft fäl Bäare, oba see send nijch aule Kjoasche. [Rempel]
There are many berries, but they are not all cherries.
Es gibt viele Beeren, aber sie sind nicht alle Kirschen.

31) Vebodne Frucht es seet. *[Epp]*
Febeedene Frucht es seet. [Rempel]
Forbidden fruit is sweet.
Verbotene Frucht ist süß.

32) Et schmaikt, oba et kost't uk. *[Epp]*
Et schmakt, oba et kostet uck. [Rempel]
It tastes good, but it costs too.
Es schmeckt, aber es kostet auch.
* With many pleasures comes a price.*

Broot un Botta.

33) Wäa daut Kuarn äte well, mott de Näät knacke. *[Epp]*
Wäa daut Kuarn äte well, mott dee Nät knacke. [Rempel]
He who wants to eat the kernel must crack the nut.
Wer den Kern essen will, muß die Nuss knacken.

34) Hunga es de baste Koch. *[Epp]*
Hunga es dee basta Koch. [Rempel]
Hunger is the best cook.
Hunger ist der beste Koch.

35) Foarmasch [Buare] kjenne aule Pl<u>oage</u> vedroage, oba kjeen Darscht. *[Epp]*
  Büare kjenne aule Pl<u>oage</u>, oba kjeen Darscht fedr<u>oage</u>. [Rempel]
  Farmers can [handle] all plagues, but tolerate no thirst.
  Bauern können alle Plagen, aber kein Durst vertragen.
   * *Many rural people like strong drink, and even Mennonite communities had their drunkards.*

36) Aules haft een Enj, bloos de Worscht haft twee. *[Epp]*
  Aules haft een Enj, blooss dee Worscht haft twee. [Rempel]
  Everything has an end, but the sausage has two.
  Alles hat ein Ende, aber der Wurst hat zwei.

37) …Oba miene Worscht haft kjeen Enj, dee hab ekj aufjebäte *[Epp]*
  ….Oba miene Worscht haft kjeen Enj, dee hab ekj aufjebäte. [Rempel]
  …. But my sausage has no end, I have bitten it off.
  …. Aber meine Wurst hat kein Ende, die hab' ich abgebissen.
   * *A funny rejoinder to the saying listed above.*

Es de Worscht goa un goot? [www.freeimages.co.uk]

38) Hast du Korn un Worscht jen<u>uag</u>, es daut fer'em Hoawst sea kl<u>uak</u>. *[E.]*
  Hast dü Korn onn Worscht jen<u>üach</u>, es daut fe' dän Hoafst sea kl<u>üak</u>. [R.]
  Have you corn and sausage enough, that is very wise for autumn.
  Hast du Korn und Wurst genug, ist das für den Herbst sehr klug.

39) Et jeiht om de Worscht. *[Epp]*
   Et jeit omm dee Worscht. [Rempel]
   It is a matter of the sausage [ie. critical, "do or die"].
   Es geht um die Wurst.
   * *Sausage is a staple among the Germanic peoples, and like bread it is a very*
      common theme in folk sayings. Even Plautdietsche poems have been written
      about sausage.

40) Et es mi gaunz Worscht. [Epp]
   Et es mie gaunss Worscht. [Rempel]
   It is completely sausage to me.
   Es ist mir ganz Wurst.
   * *Ie. "I don't care at all about it." This expression seems to contradict the concept*
      of the last one, but this is often the case with proverbs.

41) Eernst aus 'ne Jrettworscht. *[Epp]*
   Eanst aus 'ne Jrettworscht. [Rempel]
   Serious as a gruel-sausage.
   Ernst als eine Grützenwurst.
   * *A Jrettworscht is made with meat scraps combined with a grain or grits additive.*
      It was a great favorite despite containing blood, brains, fat and other marginal
      ingredients that might repel some present-day diners.

42) Lied mäaje korte Jebäde un lange Worschte. *[Epp]*
   Lied jleijche korte Jebäde onn lange Worschte. [Rempel]
   People like short prayers and long sausages.
   Leute mögen kurze Gebete und lange Würste.
   * *Often children (and some adults) have trouble waiting to say grace before*
      starting to eat.

43) Halpt daut Bea jäajen Darscht, stellt däm Hunga 'ne Worscht.
   The beer helps against the thirst, a sausage stills the hunger.
   Hilft das Bier gegen den Durst, stillt den Hunger eine Wurst.

44) Een Hundsklotje es nich de Stääd, 'ne Worscht too opptobewoahre.
      [Epp]
   Een Hunjsstaul es nijch dee Plauts, 'ne Worscht too opptobewoare. [R.]
   A kennel is not the place to store a sausage.
   Eine Hündehütte ist nicht der Platz, einer Wurst zu aufbewahren.

45) Wäms Broot ekj ät, sien Leed ekj sinj. *[Epp]*
Wäms Broot ekj ät, sien Leet ekj sinj. [Rempel]
Whose bread I eat, his song I sing.
Wess' Brot ich ess', dess Lied ich sing.

46) Kjees un Br<u>oo</u>t moakt de Backe r<u>oo</u>t. *[Epp]*
Kjees onn Br<u>oo</u>t moakt dee Backe r<u>oo</u>t. [Rempel]
Cheese and bread make the cheeks red.
Käse und Brot macht die Backen rot.

47) Broot en eene Haund, een Steen en de aundre. *[Epp]*
Broot enn eene Haunt, een Steen enn'e aundra. [Rempel]
Bread in one hand, a stone in the other.
Brot in einer Hand, ein Stein in der anderen.
* A spiteful, two-faced person.

48) Sorj di nich om onjelädne Eia. *[Epp]*
Sorj die nijch omm onnjelaigte Eia. [Rempel]
Don't worry yourself over unlaid eggs.
Kümmere dich nicht um ungelegte Eier.

49) Maun mott ahm aus een reiwet Ei behaundle. *[Epp]*
Maun mott am aus een reiwet Ei behaundle. [Rempel]
One must treat [handle] him like a raw egg.
Man muss ihm wie ein rohes Ei hehandeln.

50) Een fula Aupel moakt tieen. *[Epp]*
Een füla Aupel moakt tian. [Rempel]
One rotten apple makes ten.
Ein fauler Apfel macht zehn.

51) Broot schleiht de Hunga doot. *[Epp]*
Broot schlait dee Hunga doot. [Rempel]
Bread strikes the hunger dead.
Brot schlägt der Hunger tot.

52) Broot fe' de Welt, oba de Worscht blifft hia. *[Epp]*
Broot fe' dee Welt, oba dee Worscht blift hia. [Rempel]
Bread for the world, but the sausage stays here.

Brot für die Welt, aber die Wurst bleibt hier.
* *Charity only goes so far, if we're talking about parting with sausage.*

53) Broot kost't Schweet. *[Epp]*
Broot kostet Schweet. [Rempel]
Bread costs sweat.
Brot kostet Schweiß.

54) Een haulwet Bulkje es bäta aus kjeen Broot.
Half a loaf is better than no bread.
Halb ein Laib ist besser als kein Brot.

55) Vääl Kjääkjsches [alt. Kochs] vedoawe däm Brie. *[Epp]*
Fäl Kochs fedoawe däm Brie. [Rempel]
Many cooks ruin the hash.
Viele Köche verderben den Brei.

56) Bäta ohne Läpel aus ohne Brie. *[Epp]*
Bäta one Läpel aus one Brie. [Rempel]
Better without [a] spoon than without hash.
Besser ohne Löffel als ohne Brei.

57) Nu gohne Hopps un Brie veloare. *[Epp]*
Nu gone [alt. send] Hopps onn Brie feloare. [Rempel]
Now the hopps and mash are lost.
Nun sind Hopfen und Maische verloren.
* *In other words, everything [the whole beer or bread batch] is lost.*

58) Met de Gaufel äte, es 'ne Eah,
Met de Finjasch kjriggt maun mea. *[Epp]*
Met dee Gaufel äte, es 'ne Ea,
Met dee Finjasch kjriggt maun mea. [Rempel]
To eat with the fork is with dignity, with the fingers one gets more.
Mit der Gabel essen ist's mit Ehr; mit den Fingern kriegt man mehr.

59) En de Noot at maun de Worscht uk ohne Broot. *[Epp]*
Enn'e Noot at maun dee Worscht uck one Broot. [Rempel]
In need one even eats the sausage without bread.
In der Not isst man der Wurst auch ohne Brot.

60) Nemm waut du magst, ät waut du nemmst! *[Epp]*
   Nemm waut dü machst, ät waut dü nemmst! [Rempel]
   Take what you want, eat what you take!
   Nimm was du magst, ess was du nimmst!
   * This is often said to the children at the kitchen table. Wasting food is a sin.

61) Äte un drinkje hällt Lief un Seel toop. *[Epp]*
   Äte onn drinkje hällt Liew onn Seel toop. [Rempel]
   Eating and drinking hold body and soul together.
   Essen und trinken hält Leib und Seele zusammen.

62) Gooda Wien vedoawt de Jeldtausch, un schlaichta de Moag. *[E.]*
   Goota Wien fedoawt dee Jelttausch, onn schlajchta dee Moag. [R.]
   Good wine ruins the purse, and bad the stomach.
   Guter Wein ruiniert den Geldbeutel, und schlechter der Magen.

63) Een veakauntjet Stekj moakt daut Muul voll. *[Epp]*
   Een feakauntijet Stekj moakt daut Mül foll. [Rempel]
   A square piece makes the mouth full.
   Ein viereckiges Stück macht den Mund voll.

64) Vääl sinje, weinig schmenje, jefft een ladja Buck. *[Epp]*
   Fäl sinje, weinijch schlenje, jeft een ladje Buck. [Rempel]
   Much singing, little snaring [gobbling], gives an empty belly.
   Vielen singen, wenig schlingen, gibt ein leerer Bauch.

65) Ät waut <u>goa</u> es, drinkj waut <u>kloa</u> es!
   Eat what is done, drink what is clear!
   Ess was gar ist, trink was klar ist!
   * Practical advice to avoid illness. One should eat well-done food and drink pure
      water to avoid ingesting bacteria and parasites.

66) Goodet Jeschmack bringt Bädelsaikj. *[Epp]*
   Gootet Jeschmack bringt Bädelsakj. [Rempel]
   Good taste brings beggar-sacks.
   Gutes Geschmack bringt Bettelsäcke.
   * If one gains a reputation for exceptional cooking, all sorts of people may happen
      to "drop by."

67) Br<u>oo</u>t moakt de Backe r<u>oo</u>t. *[Epp]*
Br<u>oo</u>t moakt dee Backe r<u>oo</u>t. [Rempel]
Bread makes the cheeks red.
Brot macht die Backen rot.

68) Met Kjees un Br<u>oo</u>t litt maun kjeene N<u>oo</u>t. *[Epp]*
Met Kjees onn Br<u>oo</u>t lidet maun kjeene N<u>oo</u>t. [Rempel]
With cheese and bread one suffers no want.
Mit Käs' und Brot leidet man keine Not.

69) Uk Schwoatbroot bewoaht jääjen Hungadoot. *[Epp]*
Uck Schwoatbroot beschutst jääjen Hungadoot. [Rempel]
Even blackbread protects against hunger-death [starvation].
Auch schwarzes Brot schützt vorm Hungertod.
 * *Blackbread was regarded as inferior to whitebread, although we now know*
   that less refined flours are actually more nutritious. Coarse flours are also
   better for our intestines.

70) Eenem sien <u>Doo</u>d es een aundrem sien Br<u>oo</u>t. *[Epp]*
Eenem sien Doot es een aundrem sien Broot. [Rempel]
For one his death is another his bread.
Für einen sein Tod ist ein anderes sein Brot.
 * *Often one person's loss is another's gain.*

71) Noh däm Äte saulst du reiwe, oda dusend Schrääd moake. *[Epp]*
No däm Äte saulst dü reiwe, oda düsent Schräd doone. [Rempel]
You should rest after food, or take [do] a thousand steps.
Nach dem Essen sollst du ruhen, oder tausend Schritte tun.

72) Biem Äte saul maun frooh senne. *[Epp]*
Biem Äte saul maun froo senne. [Rempel]
One should be joyful at meal [time].
Beim Essen soll man fröhlich sein.

73) Uut een oola Topp at maun de baste Supp. *[Epp]*
Üt een oolta Topp at maun dee baste Supp. [Rempel]
Out of an old pot one eats the best soup.
Aus einem alten Topf isst man die beste Suppe.
 * *Usually with the old pot comes an experienced cook.*

74) He fingt emma een Hoa en'e Borscht. *[Epp]*
    Hee fingt emma 'ne Hoa em Borscht. [Rempel]
    He always finds a hair in the borscht.
    Er findet immer ein Haar in der Suppe.
     * He always has a complaint or a negative comment.*

75) Es de Moag saut, woat daut Hoat frooh. *[Epp]*
    Es dee Moag saut, woat daut Hoat froo. [Rempel]
    [If] the stomach is full, the heart becomes joyful.
    Ist der Magen satt, wird das Herz fröhlich.

76) Voll moakt fuul. *[Epp]*
    Foll moakt fül. [Rempel]
    Full makes lazy.
    Voll macht faul.
    * When food is abundant some people aren't inclined to work.*

77) De hungaje Buck haft kjeene Uahre. *[Epp]*
    Dee hungrijcha Buck haft kjeene Uare. [Rempel]
    The hungry belly has no ears.
    Der hungrige Bauch hat keine Ohren.

78) Eascht daut Fräte, dan kjemmt de Sittleah. *[Epp]*
    Eascht daut Fräte, dan kjemmt dee Sittlea. [Rempel]
    First comes the fodder [chow], then comes the morality.
    Erst kommt das Fressen, dann die Moral.
    * This echoes the theory of the psychologist Abraham Maslow, who believed that
      basic needs must be satified first before people can grow morally and
      intellectually. Denied these resources, people remain animalistic.*

79) Du säädst daut du 'ne Pilztje best,
    Soo sprinj em Korf! *[Epp]*
    Dü sädst daut dü 'ne Pilskje best,
    Soo sprinj emm Korf! [Rempel]
    You said you were a mushroom,
    So jump in the basket!
    Du sagtest dass du ein Pilz bist,
    So spring im Korb!
    * A challenge to live up to one's words or promises, or to do one's painful duty.
      If the mushroom jumps into the basket it will be cooked and eaten.*

80) Aule Pilztje send ätboa, oba maunche bloos eenmol. *[Epp]*
Aule Pilskje send ätboa, mau maunjche blooss eenmol. [Rempel]
All mushrooms are edible, many only one time.
Alle Pilze sind eßbar, manche nur einmal.
* *Take care, lest you be poisoned- or make a fatal choice.*

81) Woo du de Howajrett koakst, mottst du se äte. *[Epp]*
Woo dü dee Howajrett koakst, mottst dü see äte. [Rempel]
As you cooked the porridge, so must you eat it.
Wie du kochtest den Hafenbrei, so musstest du ihn essen.
* *You must accept the consequences of your actions.*

82) Waut de Foarma [Bua] nich kjant, daut at he nich. *[Epp]*
Waut dee Bua nijch kjant, daut at hee nijch. [Rempel]
What the farmer does not recognize, that he does not eat.
Was der Bauer nicht kennt, dass isst er nicht.
* *This shows both practical caution and the conservative nature of farmers, who
    have been historically reluctant to change their practices and habits.*

83) De Väälfros jraft sien eajnet Grauf. *[Epp]*
Dee Fielfros jraft sien äjnet Grauf. [Rempel]
The glutton digs his own grave.
Der Vielfrass gräbt sein eigen Grab.
* *Obesity is linked to heart attack, stroke, diabetes, and other serious health
    threats.*

84) De seetste Wiendruwe hänje aum hechste. *[Epp]*
Dee seetste Wiendrüwe henje aum hejchste. [Rempel]
The sweetest grapes hang the highest.
Die süssesten Trauben hangen am höchsten.
* *What we can't reach always seems better than what we can.*

85) Een frindeljet Jesecht es de haulwe Mohltiet. *[Epp]*
Een frintlijchet Jesejcht es haulf dee Moltiet. [Rempel]
A smiling face is half the mealtime.
Ein lächelndes Gesicht ist halb die Mahlzeit.

86) Wan de Aupetiet [Opptiet] kjemmt, dan kjemmt uk de Jesundheit.
    [Epp]
Wan dee Opptiet kjemmt, dan kjemmt uck dee Jesuntheit. [R.]

If the appetite comes, so comes the health as well.
Wenn der Appetit kommt, so kommt auch die Gesundheit.

TIARE / ANIMALS / TIERE

87) De Odla fangt kjeene Fleaje. *[Epp]*
    Dee Odla fangt kjeene Fläje. [Rempel]
    The eagle catches no flies.
    Der Adler fangt keinen Fliege.
    * A person of distinction or nobility does not stoop to engaging in petty ventures.*

88) Balende Hunj biete nich. *[Epp]*
    Balende Hunj biete nijch. [Rempel]
    Barking dogs don't bite.
    Bellende Hunde beißen nicht.

Een Hund es Maun sien basta Frint. [www.freeimages.co.uk]

89) Kjemmst äwr'em Hund,
    kjemmst uk äwr'em Zoagel. *[Epp]*
    Wan wie äwa däm Hunt kome,
    dan kjenne wie uck äwa däm Ssoagel. [Rempel]
    If we come over the dog, then we can also [go] over the tail.
    Wenn wir über dem Hund kommen, dann können wir auch über dem
    Schwanz.

90) Vääl Hunj send däm Hos sien Dood. *[Epp]*
   Fäle Hunj send däm Hos sien Doot. [Rempel]
   Many dogs are the death of the rabbit.
   Viele Hunde sind der Tod des Kaninchens.

91) 'Ne jeschonkne Schrugg kjikjt maun nich em Muul. *[Epp]*
   'Ne jeschenkjde Schrugg kjikjt maun nijch emm Mül. [Rempel]
   One doesn't look a gift horse in the mouth.
   Einem geschenkten Gaul schaut man nicht ins Maul.

92) Soo aus de Schop, soo daut Laum. *[Epp]*
   Sooaus dee Schop, soo daut Laum. [Rempel]
   As the sheep, so the lamb.
   Wie das Schaf, so das Lamm.

93) De Oss haud vejäte, daut he mol een Kaulf wea. *[Epp]*
   Dee Oss haud fejäte, daut hee mol een Kaulf. [Rempel]
   The ox has forgotten, that he was once a calf.
   Der Ochs hat vergessen, dass er ein Kalb war.

94) Met de Wilw mott maun hiele. *[Epp]*
   Met dee Wilw mott maun hiele. [Rempel]
   With the wolves one must howl.
   Mit den Wölfen muss man heulen.

95) Fercht moakt däm Wulf jrata aus he es. *[Epp]*
   Ferjcht moakt däm Wulf jrata aus hee es. [Rempel]
   Fear makes the wolf bigger than he is.
   Furcht macht der Wulf größer als er ist.

96) Een schlopenda Foss fangt kjeen Hohn. *[Epp]*
   Een schlopenda Foss fangt kjeen Hon. [Rempel]
   A sleeping fox catches no rooster.
   Ein schlafende Fuchs fangt keinen Huhn.

97) Es de Foarma [Bua] noch nich s<u>aut</u>,
   foaht he sikj een Hohnkje pl<u>aut</u>. *[Epp]*
   Es dee Büa noch nijch s<u>aut</u>,
   foat hee sikj een Honkje pl<u>aut</u>. [Rempel]
   Is the farmer still not full, he runs a little rooster flat.

Ist der Bauer noch nicht satt, fährt er sich ein Hühnchen platt.

98) De Hohn dee een Kota friee well, es verrekt. *[Epp]*
     Dee Hon, dee een Kota befriee well, es ferekjt. [Rempel]
     The rooster, that wants to marry a tomcat, is crazy.
     Der Huhn, der einen Kater heiraten will, ist verrückt.

99) Hucke de Hohns en de <u>Aikj</u>,
     kjemmt boold Frost un Winta sien Schr<u>aikj</u>. *[Epp]*
     Hucke dee Hons enn'e <u>Akj</u>,
     kjemmt boolt Frost onn Winta sien Schr<u>akj</u>. [Rempel]
     Sit the roosters in the corner, soon comes the frost and winter terror.
     Hocken die Hühner in die Eck', kommt bald Frost und Winters Schreck.

Een Hohn jefft kjeene Eia. [www.freeimages.co.uk]

100) Wan de Hohn es plaut aus een Tala,
      wea de Kjätel [Maschien] secha schwinda. *[Epp]*
      Wan dee Hon es plaut woo een Tala,
      wea dee Kjätel sekja schwinda. [Rempel]
      If the rooster is flat as a plate, the tractor was certainly faster.
      Wenn der Huhn ist platt wie einen Teller, war der Traktor sicher
      schneller.

101) Een blindja Hohn fingt uk een Korn. *[Epp]*
      Een blinta Hon fingt uck een Korn. [Rempel]
      A blind rooster will also find a corn.

Ein blindes Huhn findet auch ein Korn.

102) Wan de Hohn kjreiht opp'em Mest,
     ändat sikj daut Wada, oda et blifft aus et es. *[Epp]*
     Wan dee Hon kjreit opp däm Mest,
     endret sikj daut Wada ooda et blift aus et es. [Rempel]
     When the rooster crows on the manure, the weather changes itself or it
     remains as it is.
     Wann der Huhn kräht auf dem Mist, ändert sich das Wetter oder er
     bleibt wie er ist.
     *Proud and foolish roosters have no power despite their posturing, and neither do
      the self-important people who strut about like roosters.

103) 'Ne goode Hahn woat selde fat. *[Epp]*
     'Ne goote Han woat selde fat. [Rempel]
     A good hen seldom becomes fat.
     Eine gute Henne wird selten fett.
     * *Good laying hens may put all their excess energy into the eggs they produce.
      Sitting on the nest prevents such hens from feeding as much.*

104) Wan de Foss prädigt, pauss op fe' diene Jans! *[Epp]*
     Wan dee Foss prädigt, pauss op fe' diene Jans! [Rempel]
     When the fox preaches, watch your geese!
     Wann der Fuchs predigt, wach deine Gänse!

105) 'Ne Stinkjkaut rikt sien eajnet Nast. *[Epp]*
     'Ne Stinkjkaut rikt sien äjnet Nast. [Rempel]
     A skunk smells his own nest.
     Ein Stinktier riecht sein eigenes Nest.

106) De Fesch stinkjt vom Kopp häa. *[Epp]*
     Dee Fesch stinkjt fomm Kopp häa. [Rempel]
     The fish stinks from its head to here.
     Der Fisch stinkt von Kopf her.

107) Wan de Fesch oppwoats em Wota sprinje,
     jefft et Räajenwada. *[Epp]*
     Wan dee Fesch oppwoats emm Wota sprinje,
     jeft et Räajenwada. [Rempel]
     If the fish in the water jump upwards, there is rainy weather.

Wenn der Fisch im Wasser springt hervor, gibt es Regenwetter.

108) He es jesund aus een Fesch em Wota. *[Epp]*
Hee es jesunt aus een Fesch emm Wota. [Rempel]
He is healthy as a fish in the water.
Er ist gesund wie ein Fisch im Wasser.

109) Wäa Duuwe haft, dee haft D<u>raikj</u>,
    oba wäa Schwien haft, dee haft Sp<u>aikj</u>. *[Epp]*
Wäa Düwe haft, dee haft Dr<u>akj</u>,
    oba wäa Schwien haft, dee haft Sp<u>akj</u>. [Rempel]
Who has doves, that one has filth, but who has pigs, that one has bacon.
Wer Tauben hat, der hat Dreck, aber wer Schweine hat, der hat Speck.

110) Ea de Säaj em Schlachthuus <u>jeiht</u>,
    veseakt se et haustig met D<u>iät</u>. *[Epp]*
Ea dee Säaj enn'em Schlachthüss <u>jeit</u>,
    feseakt see et haustijch met D<u>iät</u>. [Rempel]
Before the sow goes in the slaughterhouse, she quickly tries a diet.
Vor die Sau im Schlachthaus geht, versucht sie es rasch mit Diät.

111) Wan et däm Äsel too good jeiht, jeiht he opp'em Ies. *[Epp]*
Wan et dee Äsel too goot jeit, jeit hee opp'em Iess. [Rempel]
If it goes too good for the jackass, he goes out on the ice.
Wenn der Esel zu wohl ist, geht er aufs Eis.

112) Wan et däm Äsel too leicht jeiht, daunzt he opp'em Ies. *[Epp]*
Wan et däm Äsel too leijcht jeit, daunst hee opp'em Iess. [Rempel]
When it goes too good for the jackass, he dances on the ice.
Wann es geht der Esel zu leicht, tanzt er auf dem Eis.

113) Een oola Äsel woat kjeena lowe.
Noone will praise an old jackass.
Alte Esel wird niemand loben.

114) Wäa nich dän Äsel schlone kaun, schleiht dän Sodel. *[Epp]*
Wäa nijch dän Äsel schlone kaun, schleiht dän Sodel. [Rempel]
Who can not beat the donkey, beats the saddle.
Wer nicht den Esel schlagen kann, schlägt den Sattel.

49

* Impotent rage is often redirected.

115) 'Ne Schien voll Korn es selde ohne Mies. *[Epp]*
 Eene Schien foll Korn es selde one Mies. [Rempel]
 A barn full of corn is seldom without mice.
 Eine Scheune voll Korn ist selten ohne Mäuse.
 * Every good thing or situation has its negative aspects.

116) Wan de Kaut uut däm Huus es, daunze de Mies. *[Epp]*
 Wan dee Kaut üt däm Hüss es, daunse dee Mies. [Rempel]
 When the cat is out of the house, the mice dance.
 Wann die Katze ist aus dem Haus, tanzen die Mäuse.

117) 'Ne Kaut es aus een Leew too 'ne Muus. *[Epp]*
 Eene Kaut es aus een Leew too eene Müss. [Rempel]
 A cat is a lion to a mouse.
 Eine Katze ist ein Löwe zu einer Maus.
 * Scale and perspective differ between individuals. What is trivial to one is massive
  to another.

118) De Muus es veloare, dee met de Kaut spält. *[Epp]*
 Dee Müss es feloare, dee met dee Kaut spält. [Rempel]
 The mouse is lost, that plays with the cat.
 Die Maus ist verloren, die mit der Katze spielt.

119) 'Ne Kaut, von raicht no links, bringt Jlekj. *[Epp]*
 Eene Kaut, fonn rajcht no linjsch, bringt Jlekj. [Rempel]
 A cat, from right to left, brings luck.
 Eine Katze, von recht nach links, Glück bringt.

120) Maun mott de Kaute nich em Sack kjeepe. *[Epp]*
 Maun mott dee Kaute nijch emm Sack kjeepe. [Rempel]
 One must not buy cats in the bag.
 Man muß die Katze nicht im Sack kaufen.

121) Maun schekt nich 'ne Kaut noh-huus,
 Malkj trigj too brinje. *[Epp]*
 Maun schekt nijch eene Kaut no hüss,
 Malkj trigj too brinje. [Rempel]
 One does not send a cat home, to bring back some milk.

50

Man nicht einen Kater zu hause schickt, etwas Milch zurück zu bringen.

122) Aules fe'de Kaut. *[Epp]*
   Aules fer dee Kaut. [Rempel]
   Everything for the cat.
   Alles für der Katze.
   * In other words, everything is wasted.

123) He haft de Kaut uut'em Sack jelote. *[Epp]*
   Hee haft dee Kaut üt dän Sack jelote. [Rempel]
   He let the cat out of the bag.
   Er hat die Katze aus den Sack gelassen.

124) Jesengde Kotasch läwe lang.
   Singed tomcats live long.
   Versengte Kater leben lang.
   * Having survived the fire, they know how to avoid it in the future.

125) Bäta een Spauts en de Haund aus 'ne Duuw opp'em Dack. *[E.]*
   Bäta een Spauts enn dee Haunt aus 'ne Düw opp däm Dack. [R.]
   Better a sparrow in the hand than a dove on the roof.
   Besser einen Spatz in der hand, als eine Taube auf dem Dach.

126) Si kluak aus dee Schlang un ohne Onrennlichkjeit aus de Duuw! *[E.]*
   Sie klüak woo dee Schlang onn one Onnrennlijchkjeit woo dee Düw!
                                                          [Rempel]
   Be wise like the snake and without impurity like the dove!
   Sei klug wie die Schlangen und ohne Unreinheit wie die Tauben!

127) 'Ne Schlang vedeent kjeen Metlied. *[Epp]*
   Eene Schlang fedeent kjeen Metliet. [Rempel]
   A snake deserves [earns] no pity.
   Eine Schlange verdient kein Mitleid.

128) Nu stohne de Osse aum Boarg. *[Epp]*
   Nü stone dee Osse aum Boajch. [Rempel]
   Now the oxen stand on the hill.
   Nun stehen die Ochsen am Berg.

129) Muuskje saut, Kuarnkje betta. *[Epp]*
   Müsskje saut, Kuarnkje betta. [Rempel]
   Little mouse full [sated] , kernel bitter.
   Mäuschen satt, Kernchen bitter.

130) Vääl Jeschrie un weinig Woll, säd de Hoad, aus he vesocht een
   Schwien too schäare. *[Epp]*
   *Fäl Jeschrie onn weinijch Woll, säd dee Hoad, aus hee fesocht een
   Schwien too schäare. [Rempel]*
   *Much screaming and little wool, said the shepherd, as he tried to
   shear a pig.*
   *Viel Geschrei und wenig Wolle, sagt der Schafhirt als er vesucht ein
   Schwein zu scheren.*

131) Maun saul de Schop schäare, nich schniede. *[Epp]*
   Maun saul dee Schop schäare, nijch schniede. [Rempel]
   One should shear the sheep, not cut [them].
   Man soll die Schafe scheren, nich schneiden.

132) Roop nich "Hos' bott du ahm em Sack hast! *[Epp]*
   Roop nijch "Hos" bott dü am emm Sack hast! [Rempel]
   Do not call out "rabbit" until you have him in the sack.
   Ruf nicht "Hase" bis du ihn im Sack hast!

133) Haft de Hos een dikja F<u>al</u>, kjemmt boold de Schnee opp Dack un
   Schw<u>al</u>. *[Epp]*
   *Haft dee Hos een dikja F<u>al</u>, kjemt boolt dee Schnee opp Dack onn
   Schw<u>al</u>. [Rempel]*
   Has the rabbit a thicker fur, comes soon the snow on roof and doorstep.
   *Hat der Hase ein dicker Pelz, kommt bald den Schnee auf Dach und
   Schwell.*

134) Du kaunst nich met däm Hos rane, un met de Hunj jäajre. *[Epp]*
   Dü kaunst nijch met däm Hos rane, onn met dee Hunj jäajre. [R.]
   You cannot run with the rabbit, and hunt with the dogs.
   Sie können nicht mit dem Hase laufen, und mit den Hunden jagen.
   * *You can't be on both sides, in this case be the hunter and the hunted. This
     echoes Luke 16:13, which points out the impossibility of serving two opposing
     masters.*

135) Wää Boare fange well, bruckt Honnig. *[Epp]*
    Wää Boare fange well, bruckt Honnijch. [Rempel]
    Who wants to catch bears, needs honey.
    Wer Bären fangen will, braucht Honig.
    *Used to refer to humans who require a certain incentive.

136) Foawt sikj root de Boa sien Spoa, dan wausst uk de Moot von
      schietstrempje Hunj. *[Epp]*
    Foawt sikj root dee Boa sien Spoa, wausst uck dee Moot fonn
    schietstrempijche Hunj. [Rempel]
    [If] the bear-trail is colored red, the courage of cowardly dogs also
    grows.
    Färbt sich rot die Spur des Bärs, wächst die Mut auch feigliche
    Hunde.

137) De Boa haft ahm opp'em Uah beklunjt. *[Epp]*
    Dee Boa haft am opp'em Ua beklunjt. [Rempel]
    The bear has tred upon his ear.
    Der Bär hat ihm aufs Ohr getreten.
    * This refers to someone that is tone-deaf, and has no ear for music.

138) Deel nich dän Fal opp'em Boa. *[Epp]*
    Deel nijch dän Fal opp däm Boa. [Rempel]
    Do not divide the pelt upon the bear.
    Teil nicht den Pelz auf dem Bär.
    * If the bear is still alive, talk about ownership of the fur is premature. In other
      words, don't focus on your pay if the job is still undone.

139) De Boa at dän basta Aupel. *[Epp]*
    Dee Boa at dän basta Aupel. [Rempel]
    The bear eats the best apple.
    Der Bär ißt den besten Apfel.
    * The powerful usually take the best of everything.

140) Wua et kjeene Sompe jefft, jefft et kjeene Pogge. *[Epp]*
    Wua et jeft kjeene Sompe, jeft et kjeene Pogge. [Rempel]
    Where there are no swamps, there are no frogs.
    Wo es keine Sümpfe gibt, gibt es keine Frösche.

141) Meewe en daut Laund, Onwada ver de Haund. *[Epp]*
   Meewe enn daut Launt, Onnwada fäa dee Haunt. [Rempel]
    Seagulls in the land, foul weather at hand.
    Möwen in's Land, Unwetter vor der Hand.
    * *A relevant saying for Europeans, but not for Kansans, who never encounter*
     such water fowl. Clearly, this saying predates 1874, when the first
     Mennonites arrived in central Kansas.

142) Wan de Meewe toom Laund fleaje,
       woare wi een Storm kjriee. *[Epp]*
     Wan dee Meewe toom Launt fläje,
     woare wie een Storm kjriee. [Rempel]
     When the seagulls fly to land, we will get a storm.
     Wenn die Möwen zum Land fliegen, werden wir einen Sturm kriegen

Maun fingt nich eenen Pelikan hia en Kaunsas. [www.freeimages.co.uk]

143) Wan de Waundavoagel schriggt,
       es de Winta nich soo wiet. *[Epp]*
     Wan dee Waundrefoagel schriggt,
     es dee Winta nijch soo wiet. [Rempel]
     When the migratory bird screams, the winter is not so far.
     Wann der Wandervogel schreit, ist der Winter nicht so weit.

144) Oole Väajel send schwoa too plekje. *[Epp]*
     Oolte Fääjel send schwoa too plekje. [Rempel]
     Old birds are hard to pluck.

Alte Vögel sind schwierig zu pflücken.
* Older and wiser people are harder to fool or cheat.

145) Voagel, frät oda stoaw! *[Epp]*
Foagel, frät oda stoaw! [Rempel]
Bird, feed or die!
Vogel, fress oder sterb!

146) Schlaichta Voagel, schlaichtet Ei. *[Epp]*
Schlajchta Foagel, schlajchtet Ei. [Rempel]
Bad bird, bad egg.
Schlechter Vogel, schlechtes Ei.
* If the parents are deficient, the children likely are too.

147) Raubvääjel sinje nich. *[Epp]*
Raupfääjel sinje nijch. [Rempel]
Birds of prey do not sing.
Raubvögel singen nicht.

148) Kome de Vääjel uut'em Nuade aun, es de Kold aul dichtbi. *[E.]*
Kome dee Fääjel üt'em Nuade aun, es dee Kold aul dijchtbie. [R.]
The birds arrive from the north, the cold is already nearby.
Kommen die Vögels aus Norden an, ist die Kälte schon dicht dabei.

149) Oole Krauje send schwoa too fange.
Old crows are hard to catch.
Alte Krähen sind schwer zu fangen.
* Past experience with danger aids in present-day security.

150) Eene Krauj deit nich een Winta moake. *[Epp]*
Eene Krauj deit nijch een Winta moake. [Rempel]
One crow does not make a winter.
Eine Krähe macht nicht einen Winter..

151) Wäa weet, wuarom de Jans boaft gohne. *[Epp]*
Wäa weet, wuaromm dee Jans boaft gone. [Rempel]
Who knows, why the geese go barefoot.
Wer weißt, warum die Gänse barfuss gehen.
*According to one account, a response given to children who ask a lot of
* unanswerable questions.*

152) Wan de Fleaje em Schaute späle,
   Woare wi boold dän Rääjen feele. *[Epp]*
   Wan dee Fläje emm Schaute späle,
   woare wie boolt dän Rääjen feele. [Rempel]
   When the flies play in the shadows, we will soon feel the rain.
   Wann die Fliege im Schatten spielen, werden wir bald den Regen
   fühlen.

153) De Fleaj en Iel fällt en de Malkj. *[Epp]*
   Dee Fläj enn Iel fällt enn'e Malkj. [Rempel]
   The fly in a hurry falls in the milk.
   Die Fliege in der Eile fällt in die Milch.
   * Greed and haste can bring fatal mistakes.

154) De Foarmhund, dee diene Hohns frat,
   es een schraikjlichet Huustia. *[Epp]*
   Dee Foarmhunt, dee diene Hons frat,
   es een schrakjlijchet Hüsstia. [Rempel]
   The farmdog, that eats your roosters, is a terrible house pet.
   Der Hofhund, der deinen Hühner frisst, ist ein schreckliches Haustier.

155) Bliewe de Schwaulme lang,
   Hab fe' däm Winta kjeena Bang. *[Epp]*
   Bliewe dee Schwaulme lang,
   hab fää däm Winta kjeena Bang. [Rempel]
   [If] the barn swallows stay long, have no fear of the winter.
   Bleiben die Schwalben lang, hab vor dem Winter keine Bang.

156) Habe de Kjeaj nuscht too fräte,
   dan haft de Foarma ahn je fejäte. *[Epp]*
   Habe dee Kjäj nuscht too fräte,
   dan haft dee Büa an je fejäte. [Rempel]
   [If] the cows have nothing to devour, [then] has the farmer truly
   forgotten them.
   Haben die Kühe nichts zu fressen, hat der Bauer sie je vergessen.

157) Et jefft Mensche un dan jefft et Schildkjräte. *[Epp]*
   Et jeft Mensche onn dan jeft et Schiltkjräte. [Rempel]
   There are people and then there are turtles.

Es gibt Menschen und dann gibt es Schildkröte.
   * *Turtles can be tricksters, and in old fairy tales they drown the naïve animal that*
   accepts a ride on their backs.

158) Boare un Biffel kjenne kjeen Foss fange. *[Epp]*
   Boare onn Beffels kjenne kjeen Foss fange. [Rempel]
   Bears and buffaloes can catch no fox.
   Bären und Büffel können keinen Fuchs fangen.

159) De Spand suggt Jeft, de Bie Honnig uut aule Bloome. *[E.]*
   Dee Spand suggt Jeft, dee Bie Honnijch üt aule Bloome. [R.]
   The spider sucks poison, the bee honey from every flower.
   Die Spinne saugt Gift, die Biene Honig aus allen Blumen.

160) Ekj räd von Ente, un du auntwuadst von Jans. *[Epp]*
   Ekj räd fonn Ente, onn dü auntwuadst fonn Jans. [Rempel]
   I speak of ducks, and you answer about geese.
   Ich rede von Enten, und du antwortet mit von Gänsen.

Een Kosebock haft foaken eenem stoakja Jeroch. [www.freeimages.co.uk]

161) Oole Kose lekje uk jearn Solt. *[Epp]*
   Oole Kose lekje uck jearn Solt. [Rempel]
   Old goats also like to lick salt.
   Alte Ziegen lecken auch gern Salz.

162) De Fleaje sette emma opp een moaget Pead. *[Epp]*
   Dee Fläje sette emma opp een moaget Peat. [Rempel]
   The flies always sit themselves on a thin horse.

Die Fliege sitzt sich immer auf ein mageres Pferd.
*The vulnerable are always targeted by predatory people.

163) Biem Riede leaht maun daut Peat, biem Räde dän Mensch. *[E.]*
Biem Riede leat maun daut Peat, biem Räde dän Mensch. [R.]
From riding one learns the horse, from speech the person.
Beim Reiten lernt man das Pferd, beim Reden den Menschen.

164) Schloh een doota Pead nich! *[Epp]*
Schlo een doota Peat nijch! [Rempel]
You don't beat a dead horse.
Schlag einen toten Pferd nicht!

165) Bäta bi een Uul jesäte aus met 'ne Hoftje jefloage. *[Epp]*
Bäta bie een Ül jesäte aus met eene Hofkje jefloage. [Rempel]
Better to have sat by an owl than have flown with a hawk.
Besser bei einer Eule gesessen als mit Falken geflogen.

166) De Gauns leaht de Schwon too sinje. *[Epp]*
Dee Gauns leat dee Schwon too sinje. [Rempel]
The goose teaches the swam to sing.
Die Gans lehrt den Schwan singen.

167) Waut es Soss fe' de Gauns, es Soss fe' dän Gaunta. *[Epp]*
Waut es Soss fer dee Gauns, es Soss fer dän Gaunta. [Rempel]
What is sauce for the goose, is sauce for the gander.
Was ist Soße für die Gans, ist Soße für den Gänserich.

168) Schlopende Hunj saul maun nich woake. *[Epp]*
Schlopende Hunj saul maun nijch woake. [Rempel]
Sleeping dogs should one not awaken.
Schlafende Hunde soll man nicht wecken.

169) Wan de Hund wacka es, kaun de Hoad schlope. *[Epp]*
Wan dee Hunt wacka es, kaun dee Hoad schlope. [Rempel]
When the dog is awake, the shepherd can sleep.
Wenn der Hund wach ist, kann der Hirt schlafen.

170) Uk ohne Tähne woat een Hund sien Knoaka aunfaule. *[Epp]*
Uck one Täne woat een Hunt sienen Knoaka aunfaule. [Rempel]

Even without teeth a dog will attack his bone.
Auch ohne Zähne wird ein Hund seinen Knocken angreifen.

171) Schlopenda Hunj woake.
Sleeping dogs wake.
Schafende Hunde wecken.
* Don't mess around with a dangerous thing, or you'll get hurt.

172) Stomme Hunj biete jearn.
Silent dogs like to bite.
Stumme Hunde beißen gern.
* Many of life's dangers approach quietly, without warning.

173) Een doota Hund bitt nich. *[Epp]*
Een doota Hunt bitt nijch. [Rempel]
A dead dog doe not bite.
Ein toter Hunt beißt nicht.

174) De Hund kjriggt nich waut Broot, jiedamol he prachat. *[Epp]*
Dee Hunt kjriggt nijch waut Broot, jiedesmol hee prachat. [Rempel]
The dog does not get some bread, every time he begs.
Der Hunt erhält nicht etwas Brot, jedes mal er bittet.

175) De dikja de Huppsfleaj, de denna de Hund. *[Epp]*
Dee dikja dee Huppsfläj, dee denna dee Hunt. [Rempel]
The fatter the flea, the thinner the dog.
Der dicker der Floh, der dünner der Hund.

176) Een schuchta Hund mast't nich. *[Epp]*
Een schuchta Hunt mastet nijch. [Rempel]
A timid dog does not fatten.
Ein schüchterner Hund mästet nicht.

177) Wan een Hund sien Jebäde beauntwuadt weare, wudd et Knoakes
    räajne. *[Epp]*
*Wan een Hunt sien Jebäde beauntwuadet weare, wudd et Knoakes
    räajne. [Rempel]*
If a dog's prayers were answered, it would rain bones.
*Wenn die Gebetes eines Hundes beantwortet wurden, würde es
    Knochen regnen.*

178) De Spautse piepe et von de Däakja. *[Epp]*
Dee Spautse piepe et fonn dee Däakja. [Rempel]
The sparrows whistle it from the roofs.
Die Spatzen pfeifen es von den Dächern.
* The word is out.

179) Een Leahra un een Hunt vedeene sikj daut Broot met dee Muul. *[E.]*
Een Leara onn een Hunt fedeene sikj daut Broot met dee Mül. [R.]
A teacher and a dog earn their bread with the mouth.
Ein Lehrer und ein Hund verdienen sich das Brot mit däm Mund.

180) Pead lote sikj toom Wota brinje, oba nich too drinkje bedwinje. *[E.]*
Pead lote sikj toom Wota brinje, oba nijch too drinkje bedwinje. [R.]
Horses let [one] bring them to water, but not force them to drink.
Pferde lassen sich zum Wasser bringen, aber nicht zum trinken
zwingen.

Pead send scheene Tiare. [www.freeimages.co.uk]

181) Maun mott pläaje, met de Pead maun haft. *[Epp]*
Maun mott pläje, met dee Pead maun haft. [Rempel]
One must plow with the horses one has.
Man muss pflügen, mit den Pferden man hat.
* You have to make due with the resources you have.

182) Daut Peat weet wua siene Kjrebb es.
The horse knows where his crib/manger is.
Das Pferd weiß wo seine Krippe ist.

183) Tuuschst du Pead nich om, en'e Fluss siene Medd. *[Epp]*
Tüschst dü Pead nijch omm, enn'e Fluss siene Med. [Rempel]
Do no switch horses in the river's middle.
Tauschen Sie Pferde nicht mitten in dem Fluß aus.
* After you start something, stay the course.

184) Wan daut Peat doot es, kjemmt de Howa too lot. *[Epp]*
Wan daut Peat doot es, kjemmt dee Howa too lot. [Rempel]
If the horse is dead, the oats come too late.
Wenn das Pferd tot ist, kommt der Hafer zu spat.

185) Groote Fesche fräte de Kjleene. *[Epp]*
Groote Fesche fräte dee Kjleene. [Rempel]
Big fish devour the little [ones].
Große Fische fressen die Kleinen.

186) He es kjeena Foss noch Hos. *[Epp]*
Hee es kjeena Foss noch Hos. [Rempel]
He is not fox nor rabbit.
Er ist weder Fuchs noch Hase.

187) Een oola Foss rant nich tweemol en'e Schlenj. *[Epp]*
Een oolta Foss rant nijch tweemol enn'e Schnea. [Rempel]
An old fox runs not twice in the snare.
Ein alter Fuchs läuft nicht zweimal in die Schlinge.
* With experience we avoid the pitfalls of yesterday.

188) Een schlemma Hund jeiht emma met een jerätena Pelz. *[Epp]*
Een schlemma Hunt jeit emma met een jereetena Pels. [Rempel]
A vicious dog always goes [around] with a torn pelt.
Ein böser Hund geht immer mit einem rissigen Pelz.

189) Een Pogg kaun nich sinje, aus een Nachtigaul. *[Epp]*
Een Pogg kaun nijch sinje, aus een Nachtigaul. [Rempel]
A frog cannot sing, like a nightingale.
Ein Frosch kann nicht singen, wie ein Nachtigall.

190) Wua Pogge send, doa send uk Otboare. *[Epp]*
     Wua Pogge send, doa send uck Odeboare. [Rempel]
     Where there are frogs, there are also storks.
     Wo Frösche sind, da sind auch Störche.
        * Where the vulnerable exist one will find predators.

191) Spott nich, de Uul es uk een Voagel. *[Epp]*
     Spott nijch, dee Ül es uck een Foagel. [Rempel]
     Scorn not, the owl is also a bird.
     Spott nicht, die Eule is auch ein Vogel.

192) Een Hoofiesa woat foaken een Peat vedoawe. *[Epp]*
     Een Hoofiesa woat foake een Peat fedoawe. [Rempel]
     A horseshoe will often ruin a horse.
     Ein Hufeisen wird oft ein Pferd verderben.

193) Kjeaj un Schop gohne toop, oba de Odla schwefft auleen. *[Epp]*
     Kjäj onn Schop gone toop, oba dee Odla schwefft auleen. [Rempel]
     Cows and sheep go together, but the eagle soars alone.
     Kühe und Schäfe gehen zusammen, aber der Adler steigt allein.

194) Bale schutz väa Biete. *[Epp]*
     Bale schutzt fäa Biete. [Rempel]
     Barks protect against bites.
     Bellen schützt vor Beißen.

195) Wua habe wi de Schwien toopjeheedt? *[Epp]*
     Wua habe wie dee Schwien toop jeheedt? [Rempel]
     Where have we herded the pigs together?
     Wo haben wir die Schweine zusammen gehütet?

196) Bäta een läwendja Hund aus een dootja Leewe. *[Epp]*
     Bäta een läwendijcha Hunt aus een doota Leewe. [Rempel]
     Better a living dog than a dead lion.
     Besser eine lebendiger Hund als ein toter Löwe.

197) Wäa sikj too 'ne Duuw moakt, däm fräte de Hofkjes. *[Epp]*
     Wäa sikj too 'ne Düw moakt, däm fräte dee Hofkjes. [Rempel]
     They who turn themselves into doves, they the hawks eat.

Wer sich zur Taube macht, den fressen die Falken.

198) Pauss mau opp, he es 'ne Schildkjrät! *[Epp]*
Pauss mau opp, hee es 'ne Schiltkjrät! *[Rempel]*
But watch out, he is a turtle [deceptive, veiled, in a shell]!
Aber passt auf, er ist eine Schildkröte!

199) De Schildkjrät saicht en sien Paunza, "Werklich, ekj won doch en
een groota Stääd!" *[Epp]*
Dee Schiltkjrät sajcht enn sien Pauntsa, "Werkjlich, ekj won doch enn
een groota Plauts!" *[Rempel]*
The turtle in his armor says, "Truly, I live in a really big place!"
Die Schildkröte sagt im seinem Panzer, "Wirklich, ich wohne doch in
einen großen Platz!"
* Those who never travel, and are ignorant of the wider world, misjudge the scope
of their home environment.

200) Bäta en Voagel en'e H<u>aund</u>, aus tieen aum S<u>aund</u>. *[Epp]*
Bäta een Foagel enn dee H<u>aunt</u>, aus tian aum S<u>aunt</u>. *[Rempel]*
Better a bird in the hand, than ten on the sand.
Besser ein Vogel in der Hand, als zehn am Strand.

201) Wäa schlapt fangt kjeene Fesch.
Who sleeps catches no fish.
Wer schläft fängt keine Fische.
* A German version says "Auch wenn der Angler schläft, gibt es Fische"—
"Even if the fisherman sleeps, there are fish."

202) Stomm aus een Fesch.
Mute as a fish.
Stumm wie ein Fisch.

203) Dän Hinjaschta biete de Hunj. *[Epp]*
Dän Hinjaschta biete dee Hunj. *[Rempel]*
Den Hintersten beißen die Hunde.
The dogs bite the rear-most one.

204) Daut wea de eensje Stroohaulem,
dee däm Kameel sien Rigje bruak. *[Epp]*
Daut wea dee eensje Stroo,

dee däm Kameel sien Rigje bruak. [Rempel]
That was the [single] straw that broke the camel's back.
Das war der Stroh, der dem Kamel den Rücken brach.

205) Truu nich Kaute, dee väare schmeichle un hinje krautze! *[Epp]*
Trü nijch Kaute, dee fäare schmaikjele onn hinja krautse! [Rempel]
Trust not cats, that cuddle up front and scratch from behind!
Trau nicht Katzen, die vorne schmeicheln und hinten kratzen!

206) Kjeena haft 'ne Kaut ääh Jereft en een Boom jefunge. *[Epp]*
Kjeena haft eene Kaut äa Jereft enn een Boom jefunge. [Rempel]
Nobody ever found a cat's skeleton in a tree.
Niemand hat das Skelett einer Katze in einem Baum gefunden.
  * Cats trapped in trees seem to be in a hopeless situation, but they obviously find a
    way down. This saying encourages the depressed person to "cheer up,"
    because a bleak situation is never without hope.

207) Uk kluake Fleaje send ver de Spande nich secha. *[Epp]*
Uck klüake Fläje send fäa dee Spande nijch sejcha. [Rempel]
Even wise flies are not sure in front of the spiders.
Auch kluge Fliegen sind vor der Spinne nicht sicher.

208) Wan de Wulf jefonge es, feaht he aus en Schop opp. *[Epp]*
Wan dee Wulf jefonge es, feaht hee aus 'ne Schop opp. [Rempel]
If the wolf is caught, he acts like a sheep.
Wenn der Wolf gefangen ist, stellt er sich wie ein Schaf.
  * Herman Rempel's dictionary says that "Schop" is feminine, but Jack Thiessen
    says"Schohp" is neuter; in High German "Schaf" is also neuter, which lends support to
    Thiessen's view.

209) Een Wulf em Schl<u>op</u> fong niemols een Sch<u>op</u>. *[Epp]*
Een Wulf emm Schl<u>op</u> fong niemols een Sch<u>op</u>. [Rempel]
A wolf in sleep never caught a sheep.
Ein Wolf im Schlaf fing nie ein Schaf.

210) De Kos mott grose, wua se aunjebunge es. *[Epp]*
Dee Kos mott grose, wua see aunjebunge es. [Rempel]
The goat must graze, where it is tethered.
Die Ziege muss grasen, wo sie angebunden ist.

211) Wan de Boat daut wichtigste wea, kunne de Kose prädje. [Epp]
Wan dee Boat daut wijchtijchste wea, kunne dee Kose prädje. [R.]
If the beard were most important, the goats could preach.
Wenn der Bart das wichtigste wäre, könnte die Ziegen predigen.

212) Du saulst nich daut Peat biem Schwaunz oppscherre. *[Epp]*
Dü saulst nijch daut Peat biem Schwauns oppscherre. [Rempel]
You should not harness the horse by the tail.
Du sollst nicht das Pferd beim Schwanz aufzäumen.
* Don't go about a task backwards.

213) He sodelt de Osse un spaunt de Pead. *[Epp]*
Hee sodelt dee Osse onn spaunt dee Pead. [Rempel]
He saddles the oxen and hitches [puts the yoke on] the horses.
Er sattelt den Ochsen und koppelt die Pferde.
* In other words, this person does things completely backwards.

214) Daut Peat stoawt, oba de Sodel blifft. *[Epp]*
Daut Peat stoawt, oba dee Sodel blifft. [Rempel]
The horse dies, but the saddle remains.
Das Pferd stirbt, aber der Sattel bleibt.

215) Uk de Äsel weet waut. *[Epp]*
Uck dee Äsel weet waut. [Rempel]
Even the jackass knows something.
Auch der Esel weiß etwas.
* An expression of exasperation when confronted with a really dense person. Also, don't underestimate what even the humblest mind can accomplish, or the power of basic God-given instincts.

216) Däm wellja Äsel woat mea oppjelode. *[Epp]*
Däm wellijch Äsel woat mea oppjelode. [Rempel]
The willing donkey will be loaded with more.
Dem willigen Esel wird mehr aufgeladen.

217) De Äsel drinkt Wota, wan he uk Wien draigt. *[Epp]*
Dee Äsel drinkt Wota, wan hee uk Wien draigt. [Rempel]
The donkey drinks water, when he also carries wine.
Der Esel trinkt Wasser, wenn er auch Wein trägt.

218) Däm Äsel sien Dood es een Fast fe' de Hunj. *[Epp]*
Däm Äsel sien Doot es een Fast fer dee Hunj. [Rempel]
The death of the donkey is a feast for the dogs.
Der Tod des Esels ist ein Fest für die Hunde.

219) Een Äsel beleidigt een aundra Languah. *[Epp]*
Een Äsel beleidigt een aundre Langua. [Rempel]
A jackass insults another long-ear.
Ein Esel schimpft ein anderen Langohr.
* The "pot calls the kettle black." The critic is as bad as his/her target.

220) Hast du kjeen Peat, dan bruk een Äsel. *[Epp]*
Hast dü kjeen Peat, dan bruk een Äsel. [Rempel]
Have you no horse, then use a donkey.
Hast du kein Pferd, dann gebrauch einen Esel.
* By necessity, use whatever tool you have, even if it is second-rate.

221) De Feschvoagel gauf daut Wota Schuld,
   daut he nich schwame kunn. *[Epp]*
Dee Feschfoagel gauf daut Wota Schult,
   daut hee nijch schwame kunn. [Rempel]
The fish-bird [heron] gave the water blame, that he could not swim.
Der Fischreiher gab dem Wasser schuld, das er nicht schwimmen
   konnte.

222) Aus de Voagel, soo daut Ei. *[Epp]*
Aus dee Foagel, soo daut Ei. [Rempel]
Like the bird, so the egg.
Wie der Vogel, so das Ei.
* Good people generate good things, bad people produce bad things.

223) He haft siene Frieheit aus de Hunt em Borm. *[Epp]*
Hee haft siene Well [alt.] aus dee Hunt emm Borm. [Rempel]
He has his will [freedom] like the dog in the well.
Er hat seinen Willen[Freiheit] wie der Hund im Brunnen.
* This person has no real freedom of action at all.

224) Jieda Hoad lowt sien eajnet Schopfleesch. *[Epp]*
Jieda Hoad lowt sien äjenet Schopfleesch. [Rempel]
Every shepherd praises his mutton.

Jeder Hirt lobt seine eigene Keule.
* Beware self-praise and self-serving bias. Don't be taken in.*

225) Oole Kaute ligje jearn dichtbi de Oweback. *[Epp]*
Oolte Kaute läje jearn aun dee Oweback. [Rempel]
Old cats prefer to lie next to the oven.
Alte Katze liegen gern am Ofen.
   * With age, we naturally slow down and must accommodate own physical
     limitations. Retirement is also the time to enjoy the comforts that a life-time of
     work has earned.*

226) Oole Kaute nerkje de Mies. *[Epp]*
Oolte Kaute nerkje dee Mies. [Rempel]
Old cats tease the mice.
Alte Katzen necken die Mäuse.
   *Perhaps because they have fewer teeth and less energy. Sometimes older
   gentlemen wink at and flirt with pretty young women too.*

227) En de Nacht send aule Kaute grau. *[Epp]*
Bie Nacht send aule Kaute greiw. [Rempel]
By night all cats are grey.
Bei Nacht sind alle Katze grau.

228) "Soaus maun heedt et, soo jeiht et," säd de Foarma [Bua], aus he däm
     Noba siene Jans en sien eajna Staul heed'd. *[Epp]*
   *"Soaus maun heedt et, soo jeit et," säd dee Büa , aus hee däm
   Noba siene Jans enn sien äjne Staul heeded. [Rempel]*
   *"How one herds it, that's how it goes," said the farmer, as he drove
   his neighbor's geese into his barn.*
   *"Wie man es leitet, so es geht," sagt der Bauer, als er die Nachbars
   Gänse in seiner Scheune leitete.*

229) Een Boll jefft kjeene Malkj. *[Epp]*
Een Boll jeft kjeene Malkj. [Rempel]
A bull gives no milk.
Ein Bull [Stier] gibt keine Milch.
   * This person is totally unable to produce desired result or succeed at the task.*

230) Moak nich een Eelefaunt uut 'ne Fleaj. *[Epp]*
Moak nijch een Eelefaunt üt eene Fläj. [Rempel]
Make not an elephant out of a fly.

Mach nicht einen Elefant aus einer Fliege.
* Don't exaggerate a problem, or "make a mountain out of a mole-hill."

231) Schwoate Kjeaj jäwe witte Malkj. *[Epp]*
      Schwoate Kjäj jäwe witte Malkj. [Rempel]
      Black cows give white milk.
      Schwarze Kuhe geben weiße Milch.
      * Looks can deceive. Don't rely on superficial impressions.

232) 'Ne luude Kooh jefft weinig Malkj. *[Epp]*
      'Ne lüde Koo jeft weinijch Malkj. [Rempel]
      A noisy cow gives little milk.
      Eine lärmende Kuh gibt wenig Milch.
      * People who are the most demonstrative in their promise are sometimes "all talk and no follow-through."

Kjeaj läwe en'e Häad un fräte daut Graus. [www.freeimages.co.uk]

233) He es von'ne Kooh jebäte. *[Epp]*
      Hee es fonn'ne Koo jebäte. [Rempel]
      He was bitten by a cow.
      Er ist von einer Kuh gebissen.
      * He is not entirely "right in the head." A memory of delirium caused by unknown infection? Can cows sense mental defect [and bite people behaving strangely]? Did cows carry a disease that caused madness-- not cowpox, but another virus affecting people? There is no clearcut explanation for this saying.

234) Bedwinjst du 'ne Raut en'e Aikj, dan fällt se aun. *[Epp]*
   Bedwinjst dü eene Raut enn'e Akj dan fällt see aun. [Rempel]
   Drive a rat in the corner and he attacks.
   Zwingen Sie eine Ratte in die Ecke, dann greift sie an.

235) Habe de Tiare weinja Angst, wiels se ohne Wead läwe? *[Epp]*
   Habe dee Tiare weinijcha Angst, wiels see one Wead läwe? [Rempel]
   Have the animals less fear, because they live without words?
   Haben die Tiere weniger Angst, weil sie ohne Wörter leben?

DAUT LÄWE / LIFE & EXISTENCE / DAS LEBEN

236) Oabeit moakt daut Läwe seet.
   Work makes life sweet.
   Arbeit macht das Leben süß.

[Alt.] Oabeit moakt daut Läwe rikj.
   Work makes life rich.
   Arbeit macht das Leben reich.

237) Soo es daut Läwe: hoat oba doaväa jemeen. *[Epp]*
   Soo es daut Läwe: hoat oba doafäa jemeen. [Rempel]
   [Loosely] Thus is life: hard and lowly for all its trouble.
   So ist das Leben; hart aber dafür gemein.

238) Daut Läwe es kort, de Eewigkjeit nich soo. *[Epp]*
   Daut Läwe es kort, dee Eewijchkjeit nijch soo. [Rempel]
   Life is short, eternity not so.
   Das Leben ist kurz, die Ewigkeit nicht so.

239) Daut Kjantnis es lang, daut Läwe kort. *[Epp]*
   Daut Kjantniss es lank, daut Läwe kort. [Rempel]
   Knowledge is long, life short.
   Die Kenntnis ist lang, das Leben kurz.

240) Daut Läwe es kort, de Wensche send vääl. *[Epp]*
   Daut Läwe es kort, dee Wensche send fäl. [Rempel]
   Life is short, wishes are many.

Das Leben ist kurz, die Wünsche sind viele.

241) Daut Läwe es aus een Kjindtje sien Hamd: kort un beschäte. *[Epp]*
Daut Läwe es aus een Kjintkje sien Hamd: kort onn beschäte. [R.]
Life is like a toddler's shirt: short and soiled.
Das Leben is wie ein Kinderhemd: kurz und beschissen.

242) Läwe ohne <u>Eah</u> es kjeen Läwe m<u>ea</u>. *[Epp]*
Läwe one Ea es kjeen Läwe mea. [Rempel]
Life without dignity is no more life.
Leben ohne Ehr ist kein Leben mehr.

243) Wäa däm Dood ferjcht't, dee haft daut Läwe veloare. *[Epp]*
Wäa däm Doot ferjchtet, dee haft daut Läwe feloare. [Rempel]
Who fears death, that one has lost life.
Wer den Tod furchtet, der hat das Leben verloren.

Een Boom em Winta. [www.freeimages.co.uk]

244) Läw un läwe lote. *[Epp]*
Läwe onn läwe lote. [Rempel]
Live and let live.
Lebe und lass leben.

245) Om lang too läwe, atst du aus 'ne Kaut,
un drinkst du aus een Hund. *[Epp]*
Omm lang too läwe, atst dü aus 'ne Kaut,

70

onn drinkst dü aus een Hunt. [Rempel]
To live long, you eat like a cat and you drink like a dog.
Um lange zu leben, essen Sie wie eine Katze und trinken Sie wie ein Hund.
   * *For health, eat moderately, be choosy about your food, and drink plenty of liquids. This is still sound advice today.*

246) Daut Läwe es kjeen Kjinjaspell.
Life is no children's game.
Das Leben ist kein Kinderspiel.

247) Wan daut Läwe nich es aus du wenschst,
    wensch et aus et es. [Epp]
Wan daut Läwe es nijch aus dü wenschst,
   wensch et aus et es. [Rempel]
If life is not as you wish, wish it as it is.
Wenn das Leben nicht ist wie du wünschst, wünsch es wie es ist.

248) Rennlichkjeit es daut Haulwe Läwe, un de aundre Halft es Schiet! [E.]
Rennlijchkjeit es daut Haulwe Läwe,
onn dee aundre Halft es Schiet! [Rempel]
Cleanliness is half-measure of life, and the other half is shit!
Reinlichkeit ist das Halbe Leben, und die andere Halb ist Scheiss!

JUNG UN OOLT / YOUNG AND OLD / JUNG UND ALT

249) Een jebrenntet Kjint vemeidt daut Fia. *[Epp]*
Een jebrenntet Kjint femeidt daut Fia. [Rempel]
A burned child avoids the fire.
Ein gebranntes Kind scheut das Feuer.
* *The memory of a bad experience leaves lasting reluctance.*

250) Kjleene Kjinja, kjleene Sorje, groote Kjinja, groote Sorje.
  Small children, small worries, big children, big worries.
Kleine Kinder, kleine Sorgen, große Kinder, große Sorgen.

251) Kjleene Kjinja drekje de Kjnee, groote Kjinja daut Hoat. *[Epp]*
Kjleene Kjinja drekje dee Kjnee, groote Kjinja daut Hoat. [Rempel]

71

Small children squeeze the knee, big children the heart.
Kleine Kinder drücken die Knie, große Kinder das Herz.
* Older children have greater ability to do things that break parental hearts.

252) Waut Haunskje nich leat, leat Hauns nienich. *[Epp]*
Waut Haunskje nijch leat, leat Hauns nienijch. [Rempel]
What little Hans doesn't learn, Hans will never learn.
Was Hänschen nicht lernt, lernt Hans nimmer mehr.
* Our basic characters are shaped in early childhood.

253) Toom leare es kjeena too oolt.
Nobody is too old to learn.
Zum lernen ist keiner zu alt.

254) Ella beschutst ver Dommheit nich. *[Epp]*
Ella beschutst fää Dommheit nijch. [Rempel]
Age does not protect from folly.
Alter schützt vor Torheit nicht.

255) Daut Ella es 'ne Krankheit doarom eena stoawe mott.
Age is a sickness from which one must die.
Das Alter ist eine Krankheit daran man sterben muss.

256) Wäa stoakj foaht, dee sitt daut nich;
Wäa sacht foaht, dee meent daut mott soo. *[Epp]*
Wäa stoakj foat, dee sit daut nijch;
Wäa sacht foat, dee meent daut mott soo. [Rempel]
Who drives fast,[youth?] doesn't see it;
Who drive slow,[older person?] thinks that's how it must be.
Wer schnell fährt, der sieht das nicht;
Wer langsaml fährt, der meint das muß so.

257) Wäa vääl en siene Jugend barscht't,
 dee haft em Ella nuscht too kjame. *[Epp]*
Wäa fäl enn siene Jügent barschtet,
 dee haft emm Ella nuscht too kjame. [Rempel]
Who in youth brushes a lot, has in old-age nothing to comb.
Wer viel in seiner Jugend bürstet, der hat im Alter nichts zu kämmen.

258) De Ellsta weet aum baste. *[Epp]*
Dee Ellsta weet aum baste. [Rempel]
The oldest knows best.
Der Ältester weiß am besten.

259) Eena woat oolt aus 'ne K<u>oo</u>h, un leat emma mea doat<u>oo</u>. *[Epp]*
Eena woat oolt aus 'ne K<u>oo</u>, onn leat emma mea doat<u>oo</u>. [Rempel]
One becomes as old as the cow, and learns more and more because of it.
Man wird alt als eine Kuh, und lehrt immer mehr dazu.

260) Daut Ella kjemmt nich met Mackligkjeit. *[Epp]*
Daut Ella kjemmt nijch met Macklijchkjeit. [Rempel]
Age doesn't come with ease.
Das Alter kommt nicht mit Leichtiglich.

261) Aus de Ellre sinje, soo schiepat de Jugend. *[Epp]*
Woo dee Ellre sinje, soo schiepat dee Jügent. [Rempel]
As the parents sing, so chirp the youth.
Wie die Eltern singen, so zwitschern die Jugend.
* In other words, parents must set a good example.

262) De Jugend weet nich, de Oola kaun nich. *[Epp]*
Dee Jügent weet nijch, dee Oola kaun nijch. [Rempel]
Youth knows not, the old one cannot.
Die Jugend weiß nicht, der Alte kann nicht.

263) De Jugend kaun stoawe, de Oola mott stoawe. *[Epp]*
Dee Jügent kaun stoawe, dee Oola mott stoawe. [Rempel]
The youth can die, the old one must die.
Die Jugend kann sterben, der Alte muss sterben.

264) De Jugend kjemmt nich mea. *[Epp]*
Dee Jügent kjemmt nijch mea. [Rempel]
Youth, it does not come again.
Die Jugend kommt nicht mehr.

265) Jugend es 'ne Schuld, dee sikj dagdäajlich vebätat. *[Epp]*
Jügent es eene Schult, dee sikj dachdäalijch febätret. [Rempel]
Youth is a fault that improves daily.

Jugend ist eine Störung, die täglich verbessert.

266) Uk onse Väavodasch weare nich domm. *[Epp]*
   Uck onse Fäafodasch weare nijch domm. [Rempel]
   Even our forefathers were not dumb.
   Auch unsere Väter waren nicht dumm.

267) Oola H<u>uut</u>, kolde Br<u>uut</u>. *[Epp]*
   Oolta H<u>üt</u>, kolte Br<u>üt</u>. [Rempel]
   Old hide, cold bride.
   Alte Haut, kalte Braut.

268) Oole Biee jäwe kjeen Honnig mea. *[Epp]*
   Oolte Biee jäwe kjeen Honnijch mea. [Rempel]
   Old bees give no more honey.
   Alte Bienen geben keinen Honig mehr.

269) Waut de Ellre met de Finjasch toopjekrautzt habe,
   daut schmiete de Kjinja met de Scheffel toom Fensta 'ruut. *[Epp]*
   Waut dee Ellre met dee Finjasch toopjekrautst habe,
   daut schmiete dee Kjinja met dee Scheffel toom Fensta rüt. [R.]
   What the parents scrape together with the fingers, that the children
   fling out the window with the shovel.
   Was die Eltern mit den Fingern zusammengekratzt haben, das werfen
   die Kinder mit der Schaufel zum Fenster hinaus.

270) Junget Ella es goot, oole Jugend pausst nich. *[Epp]*
   Junget Ella es goot, oolte Jügent pausst nijch. [Rempel]
   Young maturity is good, old youth is not suitable.
   Junges Alter ist gut, alte Jugend taugt nicht.
   *Precocious behavior can be good, but not immature behavior in older folks.

271) Joahre leahre mea aus Beakja. *[Epp]*
   Joare leare mea aus Bäkja. [Rempel]
   Years teach more than books.
   Jahre lehren mehr als Bücher.

272) Ver Prädjaschsähns un dolle Bolles saul eena opppausse. *[Epp]*
   Fer Prädjaschsäns onn dolle Bolles saul eena oppausse. [Rempel]
   Before preacher's sons and angry bulls one should beware.

Vor Predigers Söhnen und bösen Bullen soll man sich in acht nehmen.

273) Jung aunjewahnt, oolt jedone. *[Epp]*
Junk aunjewant, oolt jedone. [Rempel]
[If] young accustomed, old done.
Jung gewohnt, alt getan.
Early experimentation leads to old vices. The young need vigilant guidance.

274) Aus Mutta, soo Kjind. *[Epp]*
Aus Mutta, soo Kjint. [Rempel]
Like mother, like child.
So Mutter, so Kind.

275) De Nobasch äahre Kjinja send emma aum schlaichtste. *[Epp]*
Dee Nobasch äare Kjinja send emma aum schlajchtste. [Rempel]
The neighbor's children are always the worst.
Die Kinder unseres Nachbars sind immer am schlechtesten.
  * Sometimes bad luck may actually place the worst local children next door, but
    this saying also reflects parents' blindness to how unruly their own children
    are.

276) Een oola Hund es schwoa bale too leare. *[Epp]*
Een oolta Hunt es schwoa bale too leare. [Rempel]
An old dog is tough to teach to bark.
Einen alten Hund ist schwer bellen zu lernen.
  * Older people get set in their ways and resistant to innovation.

277) Vääl Jast, ladjet Nast. *[Epp]*
Fäl Jast, ladjet Nast. [Rempel]
Many guests, empty nest.
Viele Gäste, leeres Neste.
  * Exposure to many strangers can lure the children away from home.

278) Onvesocht bediedt onbedocht. *[Epp]*
Onnfesocht bediedt onnbedocht. [Rempel]
Inexperienced[untried] means unthinking.
Unversucht bedeutet unbedacht.

279) Fe' jiede Mutta äah Kind es schmock. *[Epp]*
Fe' jiede Mutta äa Kint es schmock. [Rempel]
Every mother's child is handsome.

Das Kind der jeder Mutter ist hübsch.

280) 'Ne Mutta vesteiht, waut een Kind nich saigt. *[Epp]*
   'Ne Mutta festeiht, waut een Kint nijch saigt. *[Rempel]*
   A mother understands, what a child does not say.
   Eine Mutter versteht, was ein kind nicht sagt.
   * Parents can read the smallest expression or change in posture when observing
      their children.

281) Sorje bringt graue Hoa, un Ella ohne Joahre. *[Epp]*
   Sorje bringt greiwe Hoa, onn Ella one Joare. *[Rempel]*
   Worry brings grey hair, and age without years.
   Sorge bringt graue Haare, und Alter ohne Jahre.

KLUAKHEIT UN DOMMHEIT / WISDOM & FOLLY
KLUGHEIT UND DUMMHEIT

282) Uut de Secht, uut'em Senn. *[Epp]*
   Üt dee Sejcht, üt däm Senn. *[Rempel]*
   Out of sight, out of mind.
   Aus die Sicht, aus dem Sinn.

283) Domm doaf maun senne, oba maun mott sikj too halpe weete.
   One may be dumb, but one must know how to help ones self.
   Dumm darf man sein, aber man muss sich zu helfen wissen.

284) 'Ne onjeweetende Persoon es een onwikjsta Speajel. *[Epp]*
   'Ne onnjeweetende Persoon es een onnwikjsta Späjel. *[Rempel]*
   An ignorant person is an unpolished mirror.
   Eine unwissende Person ist ein unpolierter Spiegel.

285) 'Ne Haundvoll Jeduld es bäta aus een Buschel Bräajens. *[Epp]*
   Eene Hauntfoll Jedult es bäta aus een Buschel Bräajens. *[Rempel]*
   A handfull of patience is better than a bushel of brains.
   Eine Handvoll Geduld ist besser als ein Buschel Gehirne.

286) Pracht kjemmt ver däm Faul. *[Epp]*
   Pracht kjemmt fer däm Faul. *[Rempel]*

Pride comes before the fall.
Hochmut kommt vor dem Fall.
*Proverbs 16:17 warns that "Pride goes before destruction, and haughtiness
before a fall." Most likely this is the origin of the folk expression.

287) Wäa nich heare well, mott feehle. *[Epp]*
Wäa nijch heare well, mott feele. [Rempel]
He who doesn't want to hear, must feel.
Wer nicht hören will, muss fühlen.

288) Jeff kjeena Rot, bott et aunjefroagt es.
Give no advice, until it is requested.
Gib keinen Rat, bis es verlangt ist.

289) Derch Schode woat eena kluak. *[Epp]*
Derjch Schode woat eena klüak. [Rempel]
Through tribulations one becomes wise.
Durch Schade wird man klug.

290) Jiedet Dingj haft siene twee Siede. *[Epp]*
Jiedet Dinkj haft siene twee Siede. [Rempel]
Every thing has its two sides.
Jedes Ding hat seine zwei Seiten.

291) Wäa nich twiewle kaun, es een domma Maun. *[Epp]*
Wäa nijch twiewle kaun, es een domma Maun. [Rempel]
Who cannot doubt, is a dumb man.
Wer nicht zweifeln kann, ist ein dummer Mann.

292) Wäa et nich em Kopp haft, mott et en'e Been habe. *[Epp]*
Wäa et nijch emm Kopp haft, mott et enn'e Been habe. [Rempel]
Who doesn't have it in the head, must have it in the legs.
Wer es nicht im Kopf hat, muss es in den Beinen haben.

293) Eenheit moakt stoakj.
Unity makes strength.
Einigkeit macht stark.

294) Eewung moakt dän Meista.
Practice makes the master.

Übung macht den Meister.

295) Wua et een Welle jefft, doa es uk en Waig. *[Epp]*
    Wua et een Welle jefft, doa es uck een Wajch. [Rempel]
    Where there is a will, there is also a way.
    Wo es gibt ein Will, dort ist auch ein Weg.

296) Maun heat uk dän aundra Deel. *[Epp]*
    Maun heat uck dän aundra Deel. [Rempel]
    One also hears the other part.
    Man hört auch den anderes Teil.

297) Aus du mi, soo ekj di. *[Epp]*
    Aus dü mie, soo ekj die. [Rempel]
    As you me, so I you.
    Wie du mir, so ich dir.

298) Maun kaun nich äwa sien eajna Schaute sprinje. *[Epp]*
    Maun kaun nijch äwa sien äjena Schaute sprinje. [Rempel]
    One can't jump over one's own shadow.
    Man kann nicht über den eigenes Schatten springen.

299) Aunjreff es de baste Veteidijung. *[Epp]*
    Aunjreff es dee baste Feteidijung. [Rempel]
    Offense is the best defense.
    Angriff ist die beste Verteidigung.

300) Aundre Lied, aundre Wääj.
    Other people, other ways.
    Andere Leute, andere Sitten.

301) Waut du kaunst vondoag besorje, schiffst du nich opp morje. *[Epp]*
    Waut dü kaunst fonndoag besorje, schiffst dü nijch opp morje. [R.]
    What you can attend to today, do not delay until tomorrow.
    Was du kannst heute besorgen, schiebst du nicht auf morgen.

302) Äwanacht kjemmt gooda Rot. *[Epp]*
    Äwanacht kjemmt goota Rot. [Rempel]
    Over night comes good advice.
    Übernacht kommt guter Rat.

* Sleep on a problem, and you'll have the solution by morning.

303) 'Ne Fruu äähre Tung es soo schoap aus een Massa. *[Epp]*
'Ne Frü ää Tung es soo schoap aus een Massa. [Rempel]
The tongue of a woman is as sharp as a knife.
Die Zunge einer Frau ist so scharf wie ein Messer.

304) De Tung von 'ne Fruu es ääh Schweat. *[Epp]*
Dee Tung fonn 'ne Frü es ää Schweat. [Rempel]
A woman's tongue is her sword.
Die Zunge der Frau ist ihre Schwert.

305) Wien un Fruues moake Noare von jiedrem. *[Epp]*
Wien onn Frües moake Noare fonn jiedräm. [Rempel]
Wine and women make fools of everybody.
Wein und Frauen machen Narren von jeder.

306) Denke doone Noare, kluake Lied weete aul. *[Epp]*
Denke doone Noare, klüake Lied weete aul. [Rempel]
Fools [do] think, wise people already know.
Denken tun Narren, kluge Leute wissen schon.

307) De dommste Foarmasch habe de jratste Eadschocke. *[Epp]*
Dee dommste Foarmasch [alt. Buasch] habe dee jratste Eadschocke.
    [Rempel]
The dumbest farmers have the biggest potatoes.
Die dummste Bauern haben die grösste Kartoffeln.
* Avoid excess pride in personal intelligence. Also, God blesses good but simple
   folks.

308) Kjinja un Noare räde de Woahrheit. *[Epp]*
Kjinja onn Noare räde dee Woarheit. [Rempel]
Children and fools speak the truth.
Kinder und Narren reden die Wahrheit.

309) Noare joage nenn, wua Enjel ferchte too beklunje. *[Epp]*
Noare joage nenn, wua Enjel ferjchte too beklunje. [R.]
Fools rush in, where the angels themselves fear to tread.
Narren hetzen innen, wo die Engel sich fürchten um zu treten.

310) De Frint von aulem, de Noa von kjeenem. *[Epp]*
Dee Frint fonn aulem, dee Noa fonn kjeenem. [Rempel]
The friend of everyone, the fool of everyone.
Der Freund von jedem, der Narr von allen.
* A wise person uses judgement in deciding whom to befriend.

311) Onweetenheit es de schlemmste Fähla. *[Epp]*
Onnweetenheit es dee schlemmste Fäla. [Rempel]
Ignorance is the worst mistake.
Unwissenheit ist der schlimmste Fehler.

312) Uut Fähjlasch woat eena kluak. *[Epp]*
Üt Fälasch woat eena klüak. [Rempel]
From mistakes one becomes wise.
Aus Fehlers wird man klug.

313) Waut weeh deit, leat uk. *[Epp]*
Waut wee deit, leat uck. [Rempel]
What hurts, also teaches.
Was verletzt, unterrichtet auch.

314) De kluaka Maun buut ver. *[Epp]*
Dee klüaka Maun büt fäa. [Rempel]
The wise man builds before.
Der kluge Mann baut vor.

315) En kluaka Maun, en stoakja Maun. *[Epp]*
Een klüaka Maun, een stoakja Maun. [Rempel]
A wise man, a strong man.
Ein kluger Mann, ein starker Mann.

316) De kluaka Maun haft lange Uahre un 'ne korte Tung. *[Epp]*
Dee klüaka Maun haft lange Uare onn 'ne korte Tung. [Rempel]
The wise man has long ears and a short tongue.
Der kluge Mann hat lange Ohren und eine kurze Zunge.
* In other words, the wise man listens more than he speaks.

317) Uk de Kjleakjsta kaun erre. *[Epp]*
Uck dee Klüaksta kaun erre. [Rempel]
Even the wisest one can err.

Auch der Klügste kann irren.

318) Hope un wachte moake maunche too Noare. *[Epp]*
   Hope onn wachte moake maunjche toom Noare. *[Rempel]*
   Hoping and waiting makes fools out of many.
   Hoffen und harren machen manche zu Narren.

319) Et jefft uk jeleade Noare. *[Epp]*
   Et jeft uck jeleate Noare. *[Rempel]*
   There are also learned fools.
   Es gibt auch gelehrte Narren.

320) He, dee sien eajna Leara es,
   haft en Dommkopp fe' een Student. *[Epp]*
   Hee, dee sien äjena Leara es,
   haft een Dommkopp fe' een Student. *[Rempel]*
   He, who is his own teacher, has a fool for a student.
   Er, der sein eigener Lehrer ist, hat einen Dummkopf für einen Student.

321) Et jefft uk vääl Äsels, dee mau opp twee Feet gohne. *[Epp]*
   Et jeft uck fäl Äsels, dee mau opp twee Feet gone. *[Rempel]*
   There are also many jackasses, that go on but two feet.
   Es gibt auch viele Esels, die nur auf zwei Füßen gehen.

322) Vääl weete vääl, kjeena aules. *[Epp]*
   Fäl weete fäl, kjeena aules. *[Rempel]*
   Many know much, none everything.
   Viele wissen viel, keiner alles.

323) He es mau een denna Häärinkj. *[Epp]*
   Hee es mau een denna Hearinkj. *[Rempel]*
   He is but a thin herring (a weak personality).
   Er ist nur ein dünner Hering.

324) Wäa aundre jääjat, dee mott selfst rane.
   Who hunts others, that one must himself run.
   Wer andere jagt, der muss selbst laufen.
   * *The aggressor eventually becomes a victim.*

Send Bohne werklich domm? [www.freeimages.co.uk]

325) He es domm aus Bohnestrooh. *[Epp]*
Hee es domm aus Boonestroo. [Rempel]
He is dumb as bean-straw.
Er ist dumm wie Bohnenstroh.
* This recalls the English expression "He doesn't know beans about it."

326) He haft Bohne en siene Uahre. *[Epp]*
Hee haft Boone enn siene Uare. [Rempel]
He has beans in his ears.
Er hat Bohnen in seinen Ohren.
* He cannot be reasoned with, and it is pointless to talk to him.
Proverbs 23:9 advises "Don't waste your breath on fools, for they will
despise the wisest advice."

327) He haft nich aule Bläda aum Boom. *[Epp]*
Hee haft nijch aule Bläda aum Boom. [Rempel]
He has not all the leaves on the tree.
Er hat nicht alle Blätter am Baum.

328) He es met däm Dommbiedel bekloppt. *[Epp]*
Hee es met däm Dommbiedel bekloppt. [Rempel]
He was hit with the "dumb-bag."
Er ist mit dem Dummbeutel beklopft.

329) Waut maun wenscht, jleewt maun jearn.
What one wishes, one prefers to believe.

82

Was man wünscht, glaubt man gern.

330) Wäa opp'e Ead liggt, dee beklunjt woare.
Who lies on the ground, that one will be walked on.
Wer auf den Grund liegt, der wird aufgetreten sein.

331) Dommheit un Stoltheit wausse uut een Boom. *[Epp]*
Dommheit onn Stoltheit wausse üt een Boom. [Rempel]
Folly and pride grow out of one tree.
Torheit und Stolz wachsen aus einem Baum.

332) Dommajons habe emma Jlekj.
Dummies always have luck.
Dumme haben immer Glück.

333) Kort un dikj haft kjeen Jeschekj,
Lang un denn haft uk kjeen Senn. *[Epp]*
Kort onn dikj haft kjeen Jeschekj,
Lank onn denn haft uck kjeen Senn. [Rempel]
Short and fat has no figure,
Long and thin also has no sense.
Kurz und dick hat kein Geschick,
Lang und dünn hat auch kein Sinn,

334) Wan de leewe Gott well een Noa seehne,
dan lat he däm Maun siene Fruu stoawe. *[Epp]*
Wan dee leewe Gott een Noa seene well,
dan lat hee däm Maun siene Frü stoawe. [Rempel]
If the beloved God wants to see a fool,
then he lets the man's wife die.
Wenn der liebe Gott einen Narr sehen will, dann lässt er die Frau des
Mannes sterben.
* A fool without his wife to take care of him wouldn't be long for this earth.

335) Een Noa saigt waut he weet,
un een kluaka Maun weet waut he saigt. *[Epp]*
Een Noa saigt waut hee weet,
onn een klüaka Maun weet waut hee saigt. [Rempel]
A fool says what he knows, and a wise man knows what he says.
Ein Narr sagt was er weiß, und ein kluger Mann weiß was er sagt.

336) Läajnasch bedroage sikj selwst soo vääl aus aundre. *[Epp]*
Läajnasch bedroage sikj selfst soo fäl aus aundre. [Rempel]
Liars deceive themselves as much as others.
Lügner betrügen sich selbst soviel wie andere.

337) Een kluaka Maun wählt nich de Kos aus sien Goadna. *[Epp]*
Een klüaka Maun wählt nijch dee Kos aus sien Goadna. [Rempel]
A wise man does not choose the goat as his gardener.
Ein kluger Mann wählt nicht die Ziege als sein Gärtner.

338) Rot saul ver Haundlung kome. *[Epp]*
Rot saul fäa Haundlung kome. [Rempel]
Advice should come before action.
Rat sollte vor Tätigkeit kommen.

339) Jedocht wan nichta, jesaigt wan besope. *[Epp]*
Jedocht wan nijchta, jesaikt wan besope. [Rempel]
Thought when sober, said when drunk.
Gedacht wenn nüchtern, besagt wenn betrunken.

JELD / MONEY / GELD

340) Jeld auleen moakt nich jlekjlich. *[Epp]*
Jelt auleen moakt nijch jlekjlijch. [Rempel]
Money alone doesn't make happiness.
Gelt allein macht nicht glücklich.

341) Wää däm Kopeck niche eart, es dan Rubel nich weat. *[Epp]*
Wää däm Kopeck nijch eart, es dan Rubel nijch weat. [Rempel]
Who doesn't value the Kopeck is not worth the Ruble.
Wer den Pfennig nicht ehrt, ist den Mark nicht wert.

342) Morjestund haft Gold em Muul. *[Epp]*
Morjestund haft Golt emm Mül. [Rempel]
Morning hour has gold in its mouth.
Morgenstund' hat Gold im Mund.

343) Jeld veloare, waut veloare,
   Eah veloare, väl veloare; Gott veloare, aules veloare. *[Epp]*
   Jelt feloare, waut feloare;
   Ea feloare, fäl feloare; Gott feloare, aules feloare. [Rempel]
   Money lost, something lost; Honor lost, much lost, God lost, everything lost.
   Gelt verloren, was verloren; Ehr verloren, viel verloren; Gott verloren, alles verloren.

Soo jeiht et oppe Welt, eena haft dän Biedel, de aundre haft daut Jeld.

344) Spoasaumkjeit unjastett't daut Huus. *[Epp]*
   Spoasaumkjeit unjastettet daut Hüss. [Rempel]
   Thrift supports the house.
   Sparsamkeit erhält das Haus.

345) Väasechtje Mana wähle spoasauma Fruues uut. *[Epp]*
   Fäasejchtijche Manna wäle spoasaume Frües üt. [Rempel]
   Prudent men choose thrifty wives.
   Besonnene Männer wählen genügsame Frauen.

346) Wan een Maun rikj es, fangt he aun to spoare. *[Epp]*
   Wan een Maun rikj es, fangt hee aun too spoare. [Rempel]
   When a man is rich, he begins to save.
   Wenn ein Mann reich ist, fängt er an zu sparen.

347) He haft Jeld aus Mest. *[Epp]*
Hee haft Jelt aus Mest. [Rempel]
He has money like manure.
Er hat Geld wie Mist.

348) Liehe bringt Sorje. *[Epp]*
Liee bringt Sorje. [Rempel]
To borrow brings worry.
Borgen bringt Sorgen.

349) Aules es nich Gold, daut blenkjat. *[Epp]*
Aules es nijch Golt, daut blenkjet. [Rempel]
Everything is not gold, that glitters.
Es ist nicht alles Gold, was glänzt.

350) Gold jeiht derch aule Däare buta de Himmelsdäa. *[Epp]*
Golt jeit derjch aule Däare büta dee Himmelsdäa. [Rempel]
Gold goes through every door except the door to heaven.
Gold geht durch alle Türen außer der Himmelstür.

351) Rikjdoom bringt Huachnäsigkjeit. *[Epp]*
Rikjdom bringt Hüachnäsijchkjeit. [Rempel]
Riches bring arrogance [high-nose-edness].
Reichtum bringt Arroganz.

352) Een goldna Homa braikt een iesana Puat. *[Epp]*
Een goltena Homa braikt een Iesapuat. [Rempel]
A golden hammer breaks an iron gate.
Ein goldener Hammer bricht ein Eisentor.
* Wealth can surmount normally impassible barriers.

353) De Jietzje tohlt twee mol. *[Epp]*
Dee Jietsijche tolt twee mol. [Rempel]
The greedy [person] pays twice.
Die Gierige zahlt zweimal.

354) Jeld vedoawt Karakta. *[Epp]*
Jelt fedoawt Karakta. [Rempel]
Money spoils character.
Gelt verdirbt den Character.

355) Bäta ohne Jeld, aus ohne Frind. *[Epp]*
Bäta one Jelt, aus one Frind. [Rempel]
Better without money, than without friends.
Besser ohne Geld, als ohne Freunde.

356) Daut latzta Hamd haft kjeene Fuppe. *[Epp]*
Daut latsta Hamd haft kjeene Fuppe. [Rempel]
The last shirt has no pockets.
Das letzte Hemd hat keine Taschen.
* When you are dead, you won't be taking any money with you.

357) Uut de Schuld, uut de Jefoah. *[Epp]*
Üt dee Schult, üt dee Jefoa. [Rempel]
Out of debt, out of danger.
Aus der Schuld, aus der Gefahr.

358) Jeld kjemmt too Jeld. *[Epp]*
Jelt kjemmt too Jelt. [Rempel]
Money comes to money.
Geld kommt zu Geld.
* The rich get richer.

359) Si toofräd met däm Goot, daut du hast. *[Epp]*
Sie toofräd met däm Goot, daut dü hast. [Rempel]
Be satisfied with the assets, that you have.
Sei zufrieden mit dem Gut, das du hast.

360) Oame Mensche brucke Jeld, de Doodje brucke Jebäde. *[Epp]*
Oame Mensche brucke Jelt, dee Doode brucke Jebäde. [Rempel]
Poor people need money, the dead need prayers.
Arme Menschen brauchen Geld, die Toten brauchen Gebete.

361) 'Ne oole Schuld es noch nich een Jeschenkj. *[Epp]*
'Ne oolte Schult es noch nijch een Jeschenkj. [Rempel]
An old loan is still not a gift.
Ein alte Schuld ist noch nicht ein Geschenk.

362) Wan du kjaffst, bruck de Uage, nich de Oahre. *[Epp]*
Wan dü kjafst, bruck dee Üage, nijch dee Oare. [Rempel]

When you buy, use the eyes, not the ears.
Wenn Sie kaufen, benutzen Sie die Augen, nicht die Ohren.
* Look at what you intend to buy, and don't listen to a salesmen's clever pitch.*

363) Kooplied wensche fe' hundat Uage,
Vekjeepa fe' kjeene. *[Epp]*
Kooplied wensche fe' hundat Üage,
Fekjeepa fe' kjeene. [Rempel]
Buyers wish for a hundred eyes, sellers for none.
Käufer wünschen für ein hundert Augen, Verkäufer für keine.

364) Gold moakt op aule Däare. *[Epp]*
Golt moakt op aule Däare. [Rempel]
Gold opens all doors.
Gold öffnet alle Türen.

365) De Diewel fangt de measchte Seele en een goldnet Nat. *[Epp]*
Dee Diewel fangt dee measchte Seele enn een goltenet Nat. [R.]
The devil catches the most souls in a golden net.
Der Teufel fängt die meisten Seelen in einem goldenen Netz.
* Avarice is a common pitfall for sinful humanity. The Russians say "Когда́
  де́ньги говоря́т, тогда́ пра́вда молчи́т:" [Kogda den'gi govoryat, togda pravda
  molchit.] "When money talks, the truth is mute."*

366) Jeld em Biedel [en'e Fupp] vedrifft de Truarigkjeit. *[Epp]*
Jelt emm Biedel [enn'e Fupp] fedrifft dee Trüarijchkjeit. [R.]
Money in the purse [alt. in the pocket] dispels sadness.
Gelt im Beutel zerstreut die Traurigkeit.

367) Jeld aus Hei hab ekj nich. *[Epp]*
Jelt aus Hei hab ekj nijch. [Rempel]
Money like hay have I not.
Geld wie Heu habe ich nicht.

368) Billig es kostboa. *[Epp]*
Billijch es kostboa. [Rempel]
Cheap is expensive.
Billig ist teuer.
* Buying cheap material can cost you more in the long run.*

En Gott wi vetrue. [www.freeimages.co.uk]

369) Dee, dee daut Vemeaje haft, bringt de Bruut t'huus. *[Epp]*
Dee, dee daut Femäje haft, bringt dee Brüt tüss. [Rempel]
He, who has the fortune, brings the bride home.
Der, der das Vermögen hat, bringt die Braut zu Hause.

370) Et es too lot too spoare, wan de Tausch ladig es. *[Epp]*
Et es too lot too spoare, wan dee Tausch ladijch es. [Rempel]
It is too late to save, when the purse is empty.
Es ist zu spat zu sparen, wenn die Tasche leer ist.

371) Wua et Jeld jefft, doa jefft et Frind. *[Epp]*
Wua et Jelt jeft, doa jeft et Frind. [Rempel]
Where there is money, there are friends.
Wo es Geld gibt, da gibt es Freunde.
   * *Wealth attracts friends, until the money is gone. Proverbs 19:4 warns that*
   "Weath makes many 'friends'; poverty drives them all away."

NATUA / NATURE / NATUR

372) Vääl Bäakja moake een Stroom. *[Epp]*
Fäl Bäakja moake een Stroom. [Rempel]
Many brooks make a torrent.

Viele Bäche machen einen Strom.

373) Aule Flusse rane em Mäa enenn. *[Epp]*
  Aule Flusse rane enn't Mäa. [Rempel]
  All rivers flow in the sea.
  Alle Flüße laufen ins Meer.
  * There are many ways to the same result or destination.*

374) Fe' lauta Beem sitt maun dän Woold nich. *[Epp]*
  Fe' lüta Beem sitt maun dän Woolt nijch. [Rempel]
  Not seeing the forest for all the trees.
  Vor die Bäume den Wald nicht sehen.

375) Aus de Boom, soo de Frucht. *[Epp]*
  Aus dee Boom, soo dee Frucht. [Rempel]
  As the tree, so the fruit.
  Wie der Baum, so die Frucht.
  * The parents' character is reflected in the children.*

376) De Boom mott jeboage woare, wiels et noch jung es. *[Epp]*
  Dee Boom mott jeboage woare, wiel et noch junk es. [Rempel]
  The tree must be bent, while it is still young.
  Der Baum muss gebogen werden, während er noch jung ist.
  * The character of the child must be shaped at a young age.*

377) Dee, dee Fruchtbeem plaunt't,
  doawt sikj nich op de Frucht velote. *[Epp]*
  dee, dee Fruchtbeem plauntet,
  mott nijch opp dee Frucht felote. [Rempel]
  He, who fruit trees plants, must not depend on the fruit.
  Der, der Fruchtbäume pflänzt, darf nicht auf die Frucht verlassen.

378) Wan de Wartel doot es, soo es de Boom uk. *[Epp]*
  Wan dee Wartel doot es, soo es dee Boom uck. [Rempel]
  When the root is dead, so the tree also is.
  Wenn die Wurzel tot ist, so ist der Baum auch.

379) 'Ne Hakj tweschen Frind bewoaht 'ne jreene Frintschoft.
  A hedge between friends preserves a green friendship.
  Eine Hecke zwischen Freunden erhält eine grüne Freundschaft.

380) Mest bringt Bloome.
Manure brings flowers.
Mist bringt Blumen.

381) Roose un Mäakjes veleare boold äare Bloom. *[Epp]*
Roose onn Mäakjes feleare boolt äare Bloom. [Rempel]
Roses and maidens soon lose their bloom.
Rosen und Mädchen verlieren bald ihre Blüte.

382) Uut Stachels wausse Roose. *[Epp]*
Üt Stachels wausse Roose. [Rempel]
Roses grow out of thorns.
Aus Dornen wachsen Rosen.
* Good can come out of life's obstacles and trials.

383) Et jefft kjeene Roos ohne Stachels. *[Epp]*
Et jeft kjeene Roos one Stachels. [Rempel]
There is no rose without thorns.
Es gibt keine Rose ohne Dornen.
* Every person, plan or undertaking has negative sides.

384) Je mea maun em Mest reaht, je mea stinkt maun. *[Epp]*
Je mea maun emm Mest reat, je mea stinkt maun. [Rempel]
The more one stirs in the manure, the more one stinks.
Je mehr man im Mist rührt, desto mehr stinkt man.
* The more you get involved in an unpleasant situation, the more it rubs off on
   you.

385) Scheena Morje, wolkja Dag. *[Epp]*
Scheena Morje, wolkjijcha Dach. [Rempel]
Beautiful morning, cloudy day.
Schöner Morgen, trüber Tag.

386) Noh de Wolkje kjemmt kloa Wada. *[Epp]*
No dee Wolkje kjemmt kloa Wada. [Rempel]
After the clouds clear weather comes.
Nach die Wolken kommt klares Wetter.
* If the times seem difficult now, they will get better.

387) Low een feina Dag bloos oppenowend. *[Epp]*
Low een feina Dach blooss oppenowend. [Rempel]
Praise a fine day at night.
Lob einen schönen Tag nur am Abend.
* In other words, wait until the day is done before you rate it.

Een Wotaloch es een gooda Plautz too schwame. [www.freeimages.co.uk]

388) Stelle Wota rane deep.
Still waters run deep.
Stille Wasser fliessen tief.
* Quiet individuals are often wise.

389) Aule Wota moake naut.
All waters make wet.
Alle Wasser machen nass.

390) Ebb un Flott wachte fe' kjeen Maun. *[Epp]*
Ebb onn Flott wachte fe' kjeen Maun. [Rempel]
The tide waits for no man.
Ebbe und Flut warten auf kein Mann.

391) Ju steiht daut Wota bott aum Hauls.
The water stands up to your neck.
Euch steht das Wasser bis am Hals.

This means that you are in serious financial trouble—deeply in debt.

392) Onkruut jeiht nich waig. *[Epp]*
      Onnkrüt jeit nijch wajch. [Remple]
      Weeds do not disappear.
      Unkraut verschwindet nicht.
          **Weeds (and problems) have to be pulled (confronted), and can't be wished
          away.*

393) Woo maun em Woold enenn roopt, soo roopt et uk trigj. *[Epp]*
      Woo maun emm Woold 'nenn roopt, soo roopt et uck trigj. [R.]
      If one calls into the woods, then it also calls back.
      Wie man im Wald hinein ruft, so ruft es auch zurück.
      * If you go looking for trouble, it will find you.

394) Een Boom erkjannt maun aun de Fruchte. *[Epp]*
      Een Boom erkjannt maun aun dee Fruchte. [Rempel]
      One recognizes the tree by the fruit.
      Ein Baum erkennt man an die Früchte.

395) Aus de Boom fällt, soo liggt et. *[Epp]*
      Aus dee Boom fällt, soo liggt et. [Rempel]
      As the tree falls, so it lies.
      Als der Baum fällt, so liegt er.
          ** Forces out of our control move according to their own dynamics, and must be
          accepted.*

396) Et jefft kjeen Boom, dee nich eascht een Boomkje jewäse es. *[Epp]*
      Et jeft kjeen Boom, dee nijch eascht een Boomtje jewäse es. [Rempel]
      There is no tree, that was not first a little tree.
      Es gibt kein Baum, der nicht erst ein Sproß gewesen ist.

397) Fällt de Boom biem easchta Schlag,
      wea bestemmt de Boomstaum weakj. *[Epp]*
      *Fällt dee Boom biem easchta Schlach,
      wea bestemmt dee Boomstaum wäkj. [Rempel]*
      Falls the tree at the first blow, [then] the tree trunk was certainly soft.
      *Fällt der Baum beim ersten Streich, war bestimmt der Baumstamm
      weich.*

398) Wan daut Blaut aum Boomkje blifft,
   es de Winta noch raicht wiet. *[Epp]*
   Wan daut Blaut aum Boomkje blifft,
   es dee Winta noch rajcht wiet. [Rempel]
   If the leaf stays on the little tree, is the winter still quite far away.
   Wenn das Blatt am Bäumchen bleibt, ist der Winter noch recht weit.

399) Huage Beem fange vääl Wind. *[Epp]*
   Hüache Beem fange fäl Wint. [Rempel]
   High trees catch a lot of wind.
   Hohe Bäume fangen viel Wind.
   * Likewise, people who stand out can attract trouble. For much of Mennonite
      history, keeping a "low profile" was wise.

400) Aus maun 'erut em Woold schriggt, soo schault et. *[Epp]*
   Aus maun erüt emm Woolt schriggt, soo schault et. [Rempel]
   As one screams out in the forest, so it echoes.
   Wie man heraus im Wald schreit, so widerhallt es.

401) Et jefft Ruh ver däm Storm. Alt.-- Ruh kjemmt ver däm Storm. *[Epp]*
   Et jeft Rü fää däm Storm.   Alt.-- Rü kjemmt fää däm Storm. [R.]
   There is peace before the storm.   Peace comes before the storm.
   Es gibt Ruh vor dem Sturm.   Ruh kommt vor dem Sturm.

402) Een Storm en een Wotaglaus. *[Epp]*
   Een Storm enn een Wotaglauss. [Rempel]
   A storm in a water glass.
   Ein Sturm in einem Wasserglas.

403) Je mea Blott du schmittst, je mea Ead hast du. *[Epp]*
   Je mea Blott dü schmittst, je mea Ead hast du. [Rempel]
   The more mud you throw, the more dirt you have.
   Je mehr Schlamm du wirfst, desto mehr Erde hast du.
   * You reap what you sow.

404) Maun kaun de Natua nich ändre. *[Epp]*
   Maun kaun dee Natüa nijch endre. [Rempel]
   One cannot change nature.
   Man kann die Natur nicht ändern.

405) Jäajen de Dood es noch kjeen Kruut jewosse. *[Epp]*
Jäajen dee Doot es noch kjeen Krüt jewosse. [Rempel]
Against death there is still no weed [herb] grown.
Gegen den Tod ist noch kein Kraut gewachsen.

406) Low daut Mäa, oba bliew opp däm Laund. *[Epp]*
Low daut Mäa, oba bliew opp'em Launt. [Rempel]
Praise the sea, but stay on the land.
Lob das Meer, aber bleib auf dem Lande.
* *The voyage to America by steamship convinced many immigrants to avoid future*
  sea travel. Most Mennonites from Russia had never seen the ocean, although
  some Krimmer Mennonites knew the Black Sea coast.

407) Een Hoawst, hal un kloa, es goot fe' daut komendja Joah. *[Epp]*
Een Hoafst, hal onn kloa, es goot fer daut komendja Joa. [Rempel]
An autumn, that is bright and clear, is good for the coming year.
Ein Herbst, hell und klar, ist gut für das kommende Jahr.

408) Aichte Frintschoft frisst nich em Winta. *[Epp]*
Ajchte Frintschoft frist nijch emm Winta. [Rempel]
True friendship freezes not in winter.
Echte Freudschaft friert nicht im Winter ein.
* *Even in tough times (winter) real friends remain loyal.*

409) Es de Winta <u>woarm</u>, woat de Foarma <u>oarm</u>. *[Epp]*
Es dee Winta woarm, woat dee Foarma oarm. [Rempel]
[If] The winter is warm, the farmer becomes poor.
Ist der Winter warm, wird der Bauer arm.

410) De Ruak es emma jrata aus daut Fia. *[Epp]*
Dee Rüak es emma jrata aus daut Fia. [Rempel]
The smoke is always bigger than the fire.
Der Rauch ist immer größer als das Feuer.

411) Kjeen Fia ohne Ruak. *[Epp]*
Kjeen Fia one Rüak. [Rempel]
No fire without smoke.
Kein Feuer ohne Rauch.

412) Doa spälst du met Fia. *[Epp]*
Doa spälst dü met Fia. [Rempel]

There you are playing with fire.
Da spielst du mit Feuer.

413) Owend r<u>oo</u>t, Morje g<u>oo</u>t. *[Epp]*
Owent r<u>oo</u>t, Morje g<u>oo</u>t. [Rempel]
Evening red, morning good.
Abend rot, Morgen gut.
    * Note that the rhyme only works in Plautdietsch, which means that this saying
      originated in the dialect. The same idea is expressed in the English rhyme
    "Sunset red and morning gray, sends the traveler on his way."

414) De Näwel blifft opp de Ead,
       bott de Sonn et opptraikt. *[Epp]*
Dee Näwel blifft opp dee Ead,
   bott dee Sonn et opptraikt. [Rempel]
The fog stays on the ground, until the sun pulls it up.
Der Nebel bleibt auf der Erde, bis die Sonne es hinaufzieht.

415) Wua jieda-maun jeiht, wausst daut Grauss nie. *[Epp]*
   Wua jiedamaun jeit, wausst daut Grauss nie. [Rempel]
   Where everyone goes, the grass never grows.
   Wo jeder geht, wächt das Grass nie.

416) 'Ne kjleene Wolkj vestaikt foaken de strohlendste Sonn. *[Epp]*
   Eene kjleene Wolkj festaikt foake dee strolentste Sonn. [Rempel]
   A little cloud often hides the most radiant sun.
   Eine kleine Wolke versteckt häufig die strahlendste Sonne.

417) Aprell deit waut et well.
   April does what it wants.
   April macht was es will.

418) Aprell Wada, aus 'ne Fruu äahre Leew, ändat jieda Uagenblekj. *[E.]*
   Aprell Wada, aus 'ne Frü äa Leew, endat jieda Üagenblekj. [Rempel]
   April weather, like a woman's love, changes in a moment.
   April Wetter, wie die Liebe eine Frau, ändert jeden Moment.

419) Ladj nich däm Ama bott et rääjent. *[Epp]*
   Ladj nijch däm Ama bott et rääjent. [Rempel]
   Do not empty the bucket until it rains.
   Leer nicht den Eimer bis es regnet.

Een Boom es niemols too oolt toom bääje. [www.freeimages.co.uk]

420) Groote Äkje wausse von kjleene Äkjenät. *[Epp]*
Groote Äkje wausse fonn kjleene Ätjenät. [Rempel]
Great oaks grow from little acorns.
Große Eichen von kleinen Eicheln wachsen.

421) Waut schmock bleajt, vebleajt schwind. *[Epp]*
Waut schmock bläjt, febläjt schwind. [Rempel]
What blooms beautifully fades.
Was schön blüht, verblüht schnell.

422) Wää een Goade plaunt't, dee plaunt't Jlekj. *[Epp]*
Wää een Goade plauntet, dee plauntet Jlekj. [Rempel]
Who plants a garden, that one plants happiness.
Wer ein Garten pflanzt, der planzt Glück.

423) Aus daut Feld, soo de Arnt,
Aus de Voda, soo de Sähns. *[Epp]*
Aus daut Felt, soo dee Arent,
Aus dee Foda, soo dee Säns. [Rempel]
As the field, so the crop,
As the father, so the sons.
Als das Feld, so die Ernte,
Als der Vater, so die Söhne.

LEEW / LOVE / LIEBE

424) De Leew es blind. *[Epp]*
    De *Leew es blint. [Rempel]*
    Love is blind.
    Die Liebe ist blind.

425) Kolde Hänj, woame Leew. *[Epp]*
    Kolte Henj, woame Leew. [Rempel]
    Cold hands, warm love.
    Kalte Hände, warme Liebe.

426) De Leew jeiht derch de Moag. *[Epp]*
    Dee Leew jeit derjch dee Moag. [Rempel]
    Love goes [enters] through the stomach.
    Die Liebe geht durch den Magen.

427) Wäm jefällt nich Wief, Wien un Jesang,
     Dee blifft een Noa sien Läwe lang. *[Epp]*
    Wäa jefellt nijch Wief, Wien onn Jesank,
     dee blift een Noa sien Läwe lank. [Rempel]
    Who likes not wine, woman and song, he stays a fool his whole life
     long.
    Wer liebt nicht Weib, Wein und Gesang, der bleibt ein Narr sein Leben
     lang.

428) Leew kaun Boaj schuwe. *[Epp]*
    Leew kaun Boaj schüwe. [Rempel]
    Love can shift the mountains.
    Liebe kann Berge verschieben.

429) Tiedig Kjast, lange Leew. *[Epp]*
    Tiedijch Kjast, lange Leew. [Rempel]
    Early wedding, long love.
    Frühe Hochzeit, lange Liebe.

430) Oole Leew blifft lang em Jedaichtnis. *[Epp]*
    Oole Leew blift lank emm Jedajchtniss. [Rempel]

Old love stays long in remembrance.
Alte Liebe bleibt lang im Gedächtnis.

431) Oole Leew rostat nich. *[Epp]*
   Oole Leew rostat nijch. [Rempel]
   Old love does not rust.
   Alte Liebe rostet nicht.

432) Leew äwakjemmt aules.
   Love vanquishes all.
   Liebe erobert alles.

433) Leew un Vest<u>aund</u> gohne selde Haund en H<u>aund</u>. *[Epp]*
   Leew onn Festaunt gone selde Haunt enn Haunt. [Rempel]
   Love and understanding seldom go hand in hand.
   Liebe und Verständnis gehen selten Hand in Hand.

434) Em Somma befriet maun uut Leew;
   em Winta wäajen de Woarme. *[Epp]*
   Emm Somma befriet maun üt Leew;
   emm Winta wääje dee Woarme. [Rempel]
   In the summer one marries out of love; in the winter due to the
   warmth.
   Im Sommer heiratet man aus Liebe; im Winter wegen der Wärme.

435) Jlekj em Spell, Unjlekj en de Leew. *[Epp]*
   Jlekj emm Spell, Onnjlekj enn dee Leew. [Rempel]
   Luck in [cards?] play, misfortune in love.
   Glück im Spiel, Unglück in der Liebe.

436) Een Läwe ohne Leew es aus Hund ohne Zoagel. *[Epp]*
   Een Läwe one Leew es aus Hunt one Ssoagel. [Rempel]
   A life without love is like [a] dog without [a] tail.
   Ein Leben ohne Liebe ist wie ein Hund ohne Schwanz.

437) Leew un Eia send bäta wan se fresch send. *[Epp]*
   Leew onn Eia send bäta wan see fresch send. [Rempel]
   Love and eggs are better when they are fresh.
   Liebe und Eier sind besser wann sie sind frisch.

438) Leew schmaikt seet, mau bloos met Broot. *[Epp]*
Leew schmaikt seet, mau blooss met Broot. [Rempel]
Love tastes sweet, but only with bread.
Liebe schmeckt süß, sondern nur mit Brot.
   * *Romance is hard to sustain in dire poverty.*

439) Leew ohne Jeld, Däa too Älend. *[Epp]*
Leew one Jelt, Däa too Älend. [Rempel]
Love without money, door to misery.
Liebe ohne Geld, Tür zu Elend.

440) Beoobacht de Mutta, ver du befriest daut Mäakje. *[Epp]*
Beoobachtj dee Mutta, fää dü befriest daut Mäakje. [Rempel]
Observe you the mother, before you marry the girl.
Beobacht die Mutter, bevor Sie heiraten das Mädchen.
   * *With the passage of time, many people come to resemble their parents in both appearance and behavior.*

441) Een Tuun moakt de Leew stoakja. *[Epp]*
Een Tün moakt dee Leew stoakja. [Rempel]
A fence makes love stronger.
Ein Zaun macht die Liebe stärker.
   * *Frustrated or forbidden love is made more attractive by the difficulty involved.*

442) Fia em Hoat schekjt Ruak en dän Kopp. *[Epp]*
Fia emm Hoat schekjt Rüak enn dän Kopp. [Rempel]
Fire in the heart sends smoke in the head.
Feuer im Herzen sendet Rauch in den Kopf.
   * *Love's passion offer blurs reason.*

443) Leew fangt t'huus aun. *[Epp]*
Leew fangt tüss aun. [Rempel]
Love begins at home.
Liebe fängt zu Hause an.

444) De Leew wausst met de Wied. *[Epp]*
Dee Leew wausst met dee Wied. [Rempel]
Love grows with distance.
Die Liebe wächst mit der Entfernung.

445) Folgst du de Leew, un rant se waig,
    Ranst du waig von de Leew, un folgt se. *[Epp]*
      Folchst dü dee Leew, onn rant see wajch,
        Ranst dü wajch fonn dee Leew, onn folcht see. [Rempel]
        You follow love, and it runs away,
        You run away from love, and it follows.
         Folgen Sie der Liebe, und sie flieht,
        Laufen Sie weg von der Liebe, und folgt sie.

446) Kjeen Aufgonst, kjeene Leew.
      No jealousy, no love.
      Keine Eifersucht, keine Liebe.

447) Maunche lowe, dee kjeene Leew habe. *[Epp]*
      Maunchje lowe, dee kjeene Leew habe. [Rempel]
      Many praise, who have no love.
      Viele loben, die keine Liebe haben.
       * Beware, expressions of love and praise are often empty.

448) Leew vetahlt ons vääl Sache, dee nich woa send. *[Epp]*
      Leew fetalt ons fäl Sache, dee nijch woa send. [Rempel]
      Love tells us many things that are not true.
      Liebe erzählt uns viele Sachen, die nicht wahr sind.
       * Love disrupts dispassionate, objective thought.

WEAD / WORDS / WÖRTER

449) Een Maun, een Wuat; 'ne Fruu, en Weadbuak. *[Epp]*
      Een Maun, een Wuat; eene Frü, een Weadbüak. [Rempel]
      A man, a word; a woman, a dictionary.
      Ein Mann, ein Wort; eine Frau, ein Wörterbuch.

450) Weada send Hommels ähnlich,
      dee habe Honnig un een Stachel. *[Epp]*
      Wead send Hommels änlijch,

dee habe Honnijch onn een Stachel. [Rempel]
Words are like bumblebees, they have honey and a sting.
Wörter sind Hummels ähnlich, die haben Honig und einen Stachel.

Goode Beakja send aus oole Frind.

451) Wäa eenmol liggt, däm jleewt maun nich,
uk wan he de Woahrheit rädt. *[Epp]*
Wäa eenmol liggt, däm jleewt maun nijch,
uck wan hee dee Woarheit rädt. [Rempel]
Who lies once, is not believed, [even] when he also speaks the
truth.
Wer einmal lügt, dem glaubt man nicht, und wenn er auch die
Wahrheit spricht.

452) Wan du aules jleewst, daut du lasst, bäta nich läse. *[Epp]*
Wan dü aules jleewst, daut dü lasst, bäta nijch läse. [Rempel]
If you believe everthing that you read, better not to read.
Wenn Sie alles glauben, das Sie lesen, besser nicht zu lesen.

453) Läajes send aus Schneebala.
Lies are like snowballs.
Lügen sind wie Schneebälle.

454) Läajes habe korte Been.
Lies have short legs.
Lügen haben kurze Beine.

455) De Lääj es äah eajna Rejchta. *[Epp]*
Dee Lääj es äa äjena Rejchta. [Rempel]
The lie is its own judge.
Die Lüge ist ihr eigener Richter.

456) He, dee weinig weet, saigt et schwind. *[Epp]*
Hee, dee weinijch weet, saigt et schwind. [Rempel]
He who knows little says it quickly.
Er, der wenig weiß, sagt es schnell.
   * *Those who are the quickest to blurt out a response are often the least*
   knowledgeable. The wise person listens and thinks before speaking.

457) Dien Wuat en Gott sien Uah. *[Epp]*
Dien Wuat enn Gott sien Ua. [Rempel]
Your word in God's ear.
Dein Wort in Gottes Ohr.

458) Daut Wuat, daut ruutjefloage es, fangst du nich mea. *[Epp]*
Daut Wuat, daut erütjefloage es, fangst dü nijch mea. [Rempel]
The word, that is flown out, you catch never more.
Das Wort, das ausgeflogen ist, fangst du nimmer mehr.

459) Een Maun, een Wuat.
One man, one word.
Ein Mann, ein Wort.
   * *Each person must take a position and not vacillate. Also, among equals, each*
   person's opinion holds equal weight.

460) Leewa Dote aus Weada. *[Epp]*
Leewa Dode aus Wead. [Rempel]
Rather deeds than words.
Lieber Taten als Wörter.
   * *Mennonites give behavior more credit than words, and often prefer proper action*
   over talk. "Weada" are everyday words, while "Wead" can imply more
   importance or gravity.

[Alt.] Dote saije mea aus Wead. *[Epp]*
Dode saje mea aus Wead. [Rempel]
Deeds say more than words.
Taten sagen mehr als Worte.

461) Wäa vääl schwautst, liggt vääl. *[Epp]*
Wäa fäl schwautst, liggt fäl. *[Rempel]*
Who chatters a lot, lies a lot.
Wer viel schwätzt, lügt viel.

462) Om de Sach kort too moake, schnitt maun se auf. *[Epp]*
Omm dee Sach kort too moake, schnitt maun see auf. *[Rempel]*
In order to make a [long] item [story?] short, one cuts it off.
Um die Sache kurz zu machen, schneidet man sie ab.

463) Je mea Maun last, je mea leat maun.
The more one reads, the more one learns.
Je mehr Man liest, desto mehr lernt man.

464) Groote Weada, kjleene Woakje.
Big words, small works.
Große Wörter, kleine Werke.
* Braggarts are often the least productive people.

465) Wunde von Wead send schwoa to heele. *[Epp]*
Wunde fonn Wead send schwoa to heele. *[Rempel]*
Wounds from words are difficult to heal.
Wunde von Wörter sind schwer zu heilen.

466) 'Ne schlaichte Uasoak brukt vääle Weada. *[Epp]*
Eene schlajchte Üasoak brukt fäle Wead. *[Rempel]*
A bad cause needs many words.
Eine schlechte Ursache braucht viele Wörter.
* It takes more convincing if one is selling flawed goods.

467) Waut jesaigt es, es jesaigt.
What is said, is said.
Was besagt ist, ist besagt.

468) Een gooda Rädna moakt een gooda Läajna.
A good speaker makes a good liar.
Ein guter Redner macht einen guten Lügner.

469) Met Froage kjemmt maun derch de Welt. *[Epp]*
   Met Froage kjemmt maun derjch dee Welt. [Rempel]
   With questions one gets through the world.
   Mit Fragen kommt man durch die Welt.
   * Good advice for male travelers too proud to ask for directions.*

470) Räd, soo daut ekj di seehne kaun. *[Epp]*
   Räd, soo daut ekj dee seene kaun. [Rempel]
   Speak, so I can see you.
   Sprich, also kann ich du sehen.
   * People's words can tell us more about them than their appearance.*

NOOT / POVERTY / NOT

471) Noot braikt Iesa.
   Need breaks iron.
   Not bricht Eisen.

472) Noot kjannt kjeene Jesatze. *[Epp]*
   Noot kjannt kjeene Jesatsa. [Rempel]
   Need recognizes no laws.
   Not kennt keine Gesetze.

473) Noot kjannt kjeen Jeboot.
   Need recognizes no [biblical?] commandment.
   Not kennt kein Gebot.

474) Noot leaht de Boare to daunze. *[Epp]*
   Noot leat dee Boare too daunse. [Rempel]
   Need teaches the bears to dance.
   Not lehrt den Bären tanzen.

475) Noot seakt Broot.
   Need seeks bread.
   Not sucht Brot.

476) Waut de School nich leaht, woat de Noot leahre. *[Epp]*
   Waut dee School nijch leat, woat dee Noot leare. [Rempel]

What the school does not teach, need will teach.
Was die Schule nicht lehrt, wird die Not lehren.

477) Je lenja, je schlemma, oba bäta woat et niemols.
The longer, the worse, but it will never get better.
Je länger, je schlimmer, aber besser wird es nie.

478) Frind erkjanne maun en de Noot. *[Epp]*
Frind erkjanne maun enn dee Noot. [Rempel]
Friends recognize one [another] in need.
Freunde erkennen man in der Not.

479) Oarmoot mott toofoot gohne. *[Epp]*
Oarmoot mott toofoot gone. [Rempel]
Poverty must go on foot.
Armut muss zu Fuß gehen.

480) Oarmoot koakt denne Supp. *[Epp]*
Oarmoot koakt denne Sup. [Rempel]
Poverty cooks thin soup.
Armut kocht dünne Suppen.

481) Fuulheit un Oarmoot send Nobasch. *[Epp]*
Fülheit onn Oarmoot send Nobasch. [Rempel]
Laziness and poverty are neighbors.
Faulheit und Armut sind Nachbarn.

482) Oarmoot un Hunga habe vääl jeleahde Jinja. *[Epp]*
Oarmoot onn Hunga habe fäl jeleade Jinja. [Rempel]
Poverty and hunger have many learned disciples.
Armut und Hunger haben viele gelehrnte Jünger.
  * *Many of Europe's intellectuals were notoriusly ragged and penniless.*

483) De Oarme motte daunze, soo schwind aus de Rikje piepe. *[Epp]*
Dee Oame motte daunse, soo schwind aus dee Rikje piepe. [Rempel]
The poor must dance, as fast as the rich pipe (whistle).
Die Armen müssen tanzen, sobald die Reichen pfeifen.
  * *The wealthy have unresistable power over the poor.*

484) De Oarme brucke kjeene Tausche. *[Epp]*
Dee Oame brucke kjeene Tausche. [Rempel]
The poor need no purses.
Die Armen brauchen keine Tasche.

485) De Oarme habe vääl Kjinja. *[Epp]*
Dee Oame habe fäl Kjinja. [Rempel]
The poor have many children.
Die Armen haben viele Kinder.

486) Oarme Lied habe emma Onraicht. *[Epp]*
Oame Lied habe emma Onnrajcht. [Rempel]
Poor people always have injustice.
Arme Leute haben immer Unrecht.

487) Oarmoot wenscht vääl Sache, oba Bejia mea. *[Epp]*
Oarmoot wenscht fäl Sache, oba Bejia mea. [Rempel]
Poverty wishes many things, but greed more.
Armut wünscht viele Sachen, aber Habsucht mehr.

488) Oarmoot veschaund't nich. *[Epp]*
Oarmoot feschaundet nijch. [Rempel]
Poverty disgraces not.
Armut schändet nicht.

489) Een Onjlekj kjemmt selde auleen. *[Epp]*
Een Onnjlekj kjemmt selde auleen. [Rempel]
A misfortune comes seldom alone.
Ein Unglück kommt selten allein.

490) Daut Jlekj seakje wi, daut Onjlekj seakt ons. *[Epp]*
Daut Jlekj säkje wie, daut Onnjlekj säkt onns. [Rempel]
We seek luck, misfortune seeks us.
Das Glück suchen wir, das Unglück sucht uns.

491) Een Prachasack woat nie voll. *[Epp]*
Een Prachasack woat nie foll. [Rempel]
A beggarsack never becomes full.
Ein Bettelsack wurd nie voll.

492) Vespräakje felle dän Buck nich. *[Epp]*
Fespräakje felle dän Buck nijch. *[Rempel]*
Promises do not fill the belly.
Versprechungen füllen nicht den Bauch.

493) Hunga es een gooda Rädna.
Hunger is a good speaker.
Hunger ist ein guter Redner.

494) Bäta oarm en Eah aus rikj en Schaund. *[Epp]*
Bäta oam enn Ea aus rikj enn Schaund. *[Rempel]*
Better poor in honor than rich in disgrace.
Besser arm in Ehre als reich in Schande.

495) Schlapst du em Somma, hungascht du em Winta. *[Epp]*
Schlapst dü emm Somma, hungascht dü emm Winta. *[Rempel]*
You sleep in the summer, you hunger in the winter.
Schläfst du im Sommer, hungerst du im Winter.

496) Jlekj un Glaus, woo leicht brääkje dee. *[Epp]*
Jlekj onn Glauss, woo leijcht brääkje dee. *[Rempel]*
Luck and glass, how easy that breaks.
Glück und Glas, wie leicht bricht das.

497) Een Onjlekj es kjeen Onjlekj. *[Epp]*
Een Onnjlekj es kjeen Onnjlekj. *[Rempel]*
One misfortune is no misfortune.
Ein Unglück ist kein Unglück.
* If a person has only one encounter with misfortune, complaints are unjustified.

498) Ahm steiht daut Wota bott aum Hauls. *[Epp]*
Am steit daut Wota bott aum Hauls. *[Rempel]*
The water stands up to his neck.
Ihm steht das Wasser bis am Hals.
* In other words, he is in big trouble.

499) Et jeiht nich emma, aus maun well. *[Epp]*
Et jeit nijch emma, aus maun well. *[Rempel]*
It does not always go, the way one wants.
Es geht nicht immer, wie man will.

500) Näakjstaleew sitt de Noot, nich de Uasoak. *[Epp]*
Näajchstaleew sitt dee Noot, nijch dee Üasoak. [Rempel]
Charity [neighborly love] sees the need, not the cause.
Nächstensliebe sieht die Notwendigkeit, nicht die Ursache.

501) He es oarm aus 'ne Kjoakjemuus. *[Epp]*
Hee es oam aus eene Kjoakjemüss. [Rempel]
He is poor as a churchmouse.
Er ist arm wie eine Kirchenmaus.

502) Spoa en'e Noot,
Wan du waut hast, dan frat goot. *[Epp]*
Spoa enn'e Noot,
Wan dü waut hast, dan frat goot. [Rempel]
Save in need,
When you have some, then eat good.
Spare in der Not,
Wenn du was hast, dan friss gut.

503) Noot seakt Broot, et to finje es.
Need seeks bread, where it is to be found.
Notwendigkeit sucht Brot, wo es gefunden ist.

504) Äwafluss, soo aus Noot, vedoawt vääl. *[Epp]*
Äwafluss, soo aus Noot, fedoawt fäl. [Rempel]
Abundance, like need, ruins many.
Überfluss, wie Not, ruiniert viele.

GOTT UN GLOOWE / GOD AND FAITH / GOTT UND GLAUBE

505) Oarm ooda rikj, ver Gott send aule jlikj. *[Epp]*
Oam ooda rikj, fer Gott send aule jlikj. [Rempel]
Poor or rich, all are the same before God.
Arm oder reich, vor Gott sind alle gleich.

506) Ferjcht Gott, leewet Kjind, he sitt un weet aules. *[Epp]*
Ferjcht Gott, leewet Kjint, hee sit onn weet aules. [Rempel]
Fear God, dear child, he sees and knows everything.
Fürcht Gott, liebes Kind, er sieht und weiß alles.

Dise Kjoakj es huach. [www.freeimages.co.uk]

507) Daut Feld es Gott sien Desch. *[Epp]*
Daut Felt es Gott sien Desch. [Rempel]
The field is God's table.
Das Feld ist Gottes Tisch.

508) Bi Gott es Rot. *[Epp]*
Bie Gott es Rot. [Rempel]
With God is advice.
Bei Gott ist Rat.

509) Frieheit es von Gott, Friesennigkjeit vom Diewel. *[Epp]*
Frieheit es fonn Gott, Friesennijchkjeit fomm Diewel. [Rempel]
Freedom is from God, liberality from the devil.
Freiheit ist von Gott, Freisinnigkeit vom Teufel.

510) Bi Gott es aules määjlich. *[Epp]*
Bie Gott es aules määjlijch. [Rempel]
With God everything is possible.
Bei Gott ist alles möglich.

511) De leewe Gott een Licht, de Diewel 'ne Traunlaump. *[Epp]*
Dee leewa Gott een Lijcht, dee Diewel eene Traunlaump. *[Rempel]*
The beloved God a light, the devil a blubber-lamp.
Der lieber Gott ein Licht, der Teufel eine Tranlampe.

512) Maun denkt, oba Gott lenkt. *[Epp]*
Maun denkt, oba Gott lenkt. *[Rempel]*
Man thinks, but God directs.
Mann denkt, aber Gott lenkt.

513) Seakj dien Loohn von Gott, oba nich von Mensche. *[Epp]*
Säkj dien Loon fonn Gott, mau nijch fonn Mensche. *[Rempel]*
Seek your reward from God, but not from men.
Erwart deine Belohnung von Gott, aber nicht von Menschen.

514) Bäde es nich Muulwoakj, oba Hoatwoakj. *[Epp]*
Bäde es nijch Mülwoakj, oba Hoatwoakj. *[Rempel]*
To pray is not mouth-work, but heart-work.
 Beten ist nicht Mundwerk, sondern Herzwerk.

515) Bäde un danke es de schmocksta Gottesdeehnst. *[Epp]*
Bäde onn danke es dee schmocksta Gottesdeenst. *[Rempel]*
To pray and [give] thank[s] is the most beautiful worship.
Beten und danken ist der schönste Gottesdienst.

516) Aun Gott sien Sääjen es aules jelääje.
On God's blessings is everything laid [supported by].
An Gottes Segen ist alles gelegen.

517) Halp di selwst, soo halpt di Gott. *[Epp]*
Halp die selfst, soo halpt die Gott. *[Rempel]*
Help yourself, so God helps you.
Hilf dir selbst, so hilft dir Gott.

518) Et rääjent, Gott sääjent.
It rains, God blesses.
Es regnet, Gott segnet.
* The rain itself is a godsend on the drought-prone steppes. Also, God's blessings
  shower down upon us like rain every day.

519) De Mensch läwt nich von Broot auleen. *[Epp]*
Dee Mensch läwt nijch fonn Broot auleen. [Rempel]
Man does not live from bread alone.
Der Mensch lebt nicht von Brot allein.

520) Gott siene Mähle mole langsom, oba paussend fein. *[Epp]*
Gott siene Mäle mole langsom, oba paussend fein. [Rempel]
God's mills grind slowly, but appropriately fine.
Gottes Mühlen mahlen langsam, ober trefflich fein.

521) De Oole striede äwa Gott sien Wuat, un stoawe mootloos un en
Tweiwel; de Kjinja jleewe Gott un stoawe seelig. *[Epp]*
*Dee Oole striede äwa Gott sien Wuat, onn stoawe mootlooss onn enn
Twiewel; dee Kjinja jleewe Gott onn stoawe seelijch. [Rempel]*
*The old dispute God's word, and die dispondent and in doubt; the
children believe God and die blessed.*
*Die Alte disputieren über Gottes Wort, und sterben kleinmütig und in
Zweiffel; die Kinder glauben Gott und sterben selig.*

522) Wan de Noot aum jratste es, es onsa Gott aum nääkjste. *[Epp]*
Wan dee Noot aum jratsta es, es onse Gott aum nääjchsta. [R.]
When the need is greatest, is our God the nearest.
Wenn die Not am größten ist, ist unser Gott am nächsten.

523) Jefft Gott Hoskjes, jefft he uk Grauskje. *[Epp]*
Jeft Gott Hoskjes, jeft hee uck Grauskje. [Rempel]
[If] God gives little rabbits, he also gives [new] grass.
Gibt Gott Häschen, gibt er auch Gräschen.

524) Jefft de leewe Gott Junges, jefft he uk Bexe. *[Epp]*
Jeft dee leewe Gott Junges, jeft hee uck Bekjse. [Rempel]
If the dear God gives boys, he also gives trousers.
Gibt der liebe Gott Jungen, gibt er auch Hosen.

525) Oarm un rikj es bi Gott aules jlikj. *[Epp]*
Oam onn rikj es bie Gott aules jlikj. [Rempel]
Rich and poor is all the same with God.
Arm und reich ist bei Gott alles gleich.

526) Gott halpt däm, dee sikj selwst vebäätat. *[Epp]*
Gott halpt däm, dee sikj selfst febätet. [Rempel]
He, who improves [himself], God helps.
Er, der verbessert, Gott hilft.

527) Bloos Moot! De Har Gott verohdt di nich, daut Schwien frat di nich.
    [Epp]
*Blooss Moot! Dee Har Gott ferodt die nijch, daut Schwien frat die
nijch. [Rempel]*
*Just courage! The Lord God betrays you not, the swine devours you
not.*
*Nur Mut! Der Herrgott verrät dich nicht, das Schwein frisst dich
nicht.*

528) De Har Gott haft ons twee Uahre, oba bloos eene Tung jejäwt. *[Epp]*
Dee Har Gott haft ons twee Uare, oba blooss eene Tung jejäwt. [R.]
The Lord God has given us two ears, but only one tongue.
Der Herrgott hat uns zwei Ohren, aber nur eine Zunge gegeben.
   * This implies that listening is twice as good as talking.

529) Busse es daut Hoat äahre Medizien. *[Epp]*
Büsse es daut Hoat äare Meditsien. [Rempel]
Repentence is the heart's medicine.
Reue ist die Medizin des Herzes.

530) Et bade nich aule, dee en'e Kjoakj gohne. *[Epp]*
Et bade nijch aule, dee enn'e Kjoakj gone. [Rempel]
Not everyone prays, that goes in the church.
Es beten nicht alle, die in die Kirche gehen.

531) Lostig jeläwt un seelig jestoawe, heet däm Diewel daut Spell vedoawe.
    [Epp]
*Lostijch jeläwt onn seelijch jestoawe, heet däm Diewel daut Spell
fedoawe. [Rempel]*
Joyful lived and blessed dead, calls the devil the game spoiled.
*Lustig gelebt und selig gestorben, heißt dem Teufel das Spiel
verdorben.*

532) En de Noot, frat de Diewel Fleaje. *[Epp]*
Enn dee Noot, frat dee Diewel Fläje. [Rempel]

[When] in need, the devil eats flies.
In der Not, frisst der Teufel Fliegen.

533) Mohl nich dän Diewel aun de Waund. *[Epp]*
Mol nijch dän Diewel aun dee Waunt. [Rempel]
Do not paint the devil on the wall.
Mal nicht den Teufel an der Wand.

534) De Diewel schitt emma opp de jratsta Hupe. *[Epp]*
Dee Diewel schitt emma opp dee jratsta Hüpe. [Rempel]
The devil always craps on the biggest pile.
Der Teufel scheißt immer auf die größte Haufen.

535) Wan Gott saigt "vondoag," de Diewel saigt "morje." *[Epp]*
Wan Gott saigt "fonndoag," dee Diewel saigt "morje." [Rempel]
When God says today, the Devil says tomorrow.
Wann Gott sagt heute, der Teufel sagt morgen.

536) Wan een Maun sikj reffelt, frintelt de Diewel. *[Epp]*
Wan een Maun sikj reffelt, frintelt dee Diewel. [Rempel]
When a man hurries himself, the devil smiles.
Wenn ein Mann sich beeilt, lächelt der Teufel.
* Haste results in error, and a failure to weigh the morality of one's action.

537) Aule goode Dinja send dree.
All good things are three [come in threes].
Alle gute Dinge sind drei.
* The Bible contains numerous examples of "threes." These include the trinity and Christ's resurrection on the third day after the crucifition. Tradition (but not the gospels) also marks the number of the Magi at three.

538) Adam aut dän Aupel, un onse Tähne riete noch. *[Epp]*
Adam aut dän Aupel, onn onse Täne riete noch. [Rempel]
Adam ate the apple, and our teeth still ache.
Adam aß den Apfel, und unsere Zähne schmerzen noch.

539) Wäm Gott daut Aumt jefft,
Däm jefft he uk Vestaund. *[Epp]*
Wäm Gott daut Aumt jeft,
Däm jeft hee uck Festaunt. [Rempel]

Who God gives the job,
That one he also gives understanding.
Wem Gott gibt das Amt,
Dem gibt er auch Verstand.

540) Fangst du aun to spenne, dan woat Gott dän Twearm jäwe. *[Epp]*
Fangst dü aun too spenne, dan woat Gott dän Twearm jäwe. [Rempel]
Begin to weave, and God will give the thread.
Fangen Sie an zu spinnen, und Gott wird das Gewinde geben.

541) Wan Gott hoatet Broot jefft, jefft he uk schoape Tähne. *[Epp]*
Wan Gott hoatet Broot jeft, jeft hee uck schoape Täne. [Rempel]
When God gives hard bread, he also gives sharp teeth.
Wenn Gott gibt hartes Brot, gibt er auch scharfe Zähne.
* God gives us the resources to deal with life's trials.

542) Gott heelt de Kranke, un de Dokta kjriggt daut Jeld. *[Epp]*
Gott heelt dee Kranke, onn dee Dokta kjriggt daut Jelt. [Rempel]
God cures the sick, and the doctor receives the money.
Gott heilt die Kranken, und der Arzt erhält das Geld.

543) Gooda Gloowe stool de Kooh. *[Epp]*
Gooda Gloowe stool dee Koo. [Rempel]
Good faith stole the cow.
Guter Glaube stahl die Kuh.
* Bad deeds are often done in good faith or with good intentions.

544) Tahl diene Sääjen! *[Epp]*
Tal diene Sääjen! [Rempel]
Count your blessings!
Zähl deine Segen!

545) Vejääw du sikj nuscht, oba aundre vääl. [Epp]
Fejäw dü sikj nuscht, oba aundre fäl. [Rempel]
Forgive yourself nothing, but others much.
Verzeih dich selbst nichts, aber anderen viel.

546) Wäa nich jeradt senne well, bruckt kjeen Prädja. *[Epp]*
Wäa nijch jeradt senne well, bruckt kjeen Prädja. [Rempel]
Who does not want to be saved, needs no preacher.

Wer nicht geredet sein will, braucht keinen Prediger.

547) Maun deit Iebel jenuag, wan maun kjeen Goots deit. *[Epp]*
Maun deit Iebel jenüach, wan maun kjeen Goots deit. [Rempel]
One does evil enough, when one does no good things.
Man tut Übel genug, wenn man kein Gutes tut.

548) Piljasch kome selde aus Heilja noh-huus. *[Epp]*
Piljasch kome selde aus Heilja no Hüss. [Rempel]
Pilgrims seldom come home as saints.
Pilgers kommen selten als Heiligen nach Hause.

549) Aus een Maun denkt, soo es he. *[Epp]*
Aus een Maun denkt, soo es hee. [Rempel]
As a man thinks, so is he.
Wie er denkt in dem Kopf, so ist er.

WÄA / WHO / WER

550) Wäa toolatzt lacht, lacht aum baste. *[Epp]*
Wäa toolatst lacht, lacht aum baste. [Rempel]
Who laughs last, laughs the best.
Wer zuletzt lacht, lacht am besten.

551) Wäa "A" saigt, mott uk "B" saije. *[Epp]*
Wäa "A" saigt, mott uck "B" saije. [Rempel]
Who says "A," must also say "B."
Wer "A" sagt, muss auch "B" sagen.

552) Wäa nich fuat jeiht, kjemmt niemols noh-huus. *[Epp]*
Wäa nijch fuat jeit, kjemt niemols no Hüss. [Rempel]
Who doesn't go forth, never comes home.
Wer nicht fort geht, kommt nie nach Hause.

553) Wäa dän Schode haft, brukt nich fe' dän Spott to sorje. *[Epp]*
Wäa dän Schode haft, brukt nijch fer dän Spott too sorje. [Rempel]
Who has injuries, need not worry about [mere] mockery.

Wer den Schade hat, braucht nicht vor den Spotterei zu sorgen.

554) Wäa em Glaushuus sett saul nich Steena schmiete. *[Epp]*
Wäa emm Glausshüss sett saul nijch Steena schmiete. [Rempel]
Who sits in the glass house should not fling stones.
Wer im Glashaus sitzt soll nicht Steine schmeißen.

555) Wäa goot schmäat, dee foahrt goot.
Who greases well, drives well.
Wer gut schmiert, der fährt gut.

556) Wäa nuscht deit, vedoawt uk nuscht. *[Epp]*
Wäa nuscht deit, fedoawt uck nuscht. [Rempel]
Who does nothing, spoils nothing.
Wer nichts tut, verdirbt nichts.

557) Wäa dän Dood fercht, haft daut Läwe veloare. *[Epp]*
Wäa dän Doot ferjcht, haft daut Läwe feloare. [Rempel]
Who fears death, has lost life.
Wer den Tod fürchten, hat das Leben verloren.

558) Wäa ruht, dee rostat.
Who rests, rusts.
Wer ruht, der rostet.

559) Wäa de Utwohl haft, haft de Kwol. *[Epp]*
Wäa dee Ütwol haft, haft dee Kwol. [Rempel]
Who has the choice, has the agony.
Wer die Wahl hat, hat die Qual.

560) Wäa eascht kjemmt, mohlt eascht. *[Epp]*
Wäa eascht kjemt, mohlt eascht. [Rempel]
Who comes first, mills first.
Wer erst kommt, mahlt erst.

561) Wäa schleiht, woat jeschloage.
Who hits, will be hit.
Wer schlägt, wird geschlagen.

562) Wäa plaunt't, dee ernt't.
Who plants, that one harvests.
Wer pflanzt, der mäht.

Een Foarma brukt goode Jesundheit om siene Oabeit too doone. [www.freeimages.co.uk]

563) Wäa boaft jeiht, saul kjeene Stachels seihe. *[Epp]*
Wäa boaft jeit, saul kjeene Stachels seie. [Rempel]
Who goes barefoot, should sow no thorns.
Wer barfuß geht, soll keine Dornen säen.

564) Wäa sikj opp aundre velat, dee blifft velohte. *[Epp]*
Wäa sikj opp aundre felat, dee blifft felote. [Rempel]
Who relies on others, is foresaken.
Wer sich auf andere verlässt, der bleibt verlassen.

565) Wäa too vääl leahre well, dee leaht nuscht. *[Epp]*
Wäa too fäl leare well, dee leat nuscht. [Rempel]
Who wants to learn too much, that one learns nothing.
Wer zu viel lernen will, der lernt nichts.

566) Wäa lang schlapt un schwind foaht, kjemmt uk toom Moakjt. *[Epp]*
Wäa lank schlapt onn schwind foat, kjemt uck toom Moakjt. [Rempel]
Who sleeps long and drives fast, also comes to the market.
Wer lange schläft und schnell fährt, kommt auch zum Markt.

567) Wäa habe well, dee mott growe.
   Who wants to have, must dig [toil].
   Wer haben will, der muss graben.

568) Wäa doa seakt, dee fingt.
   Who seeks, finds.
   Wer da sucht, der findet.

569) Wäa Botta opp sien Kopp haft, mott uut de Sonn bliewe. *[Epp]*
   Wäa Botta opp sien Kopp haft, mott üt dee Sonn bliewe. [Rempel]
   Who has butter on his head, must stay out of the sun.
   Wer Butter auf sein Kopf hat, muss aus die Sonne bleiben.

570) Wäa nuscht well, dee haft aules.
   Who wants nothing, has everything.
   Wer nichts will, der hat alles.

571) Wäa too mi jefft, dee leaht mi too jääwe. *[Epp]*
   Wäa too mie jeft, dee leat mie too jäwe. [Rempel]
   Who gives to me, teaches me to give.
   Wer gibt zu mir, der lehrt mich zu geben.
   * *Kind behavior spreads by example. Mennonites have always put stock in*
   Christian behavior as opposed to peoples' words or rhetoric.

572) Wäa too de Oarme jefft, lieht toom Har. *[Epp]*
   Wäa too dee Oame jeft, lieht toom Har. [Rempel]
   Who gives to the poor, lends to the Lord.
   Wer zu den Armen gibt, verleiht zum Herrn.
   * *In other words, the Lord will (more than) repay these good deeds.*

573) Wäa tiedig oppsteiht, kjemmt too waut. *[Epp]*
   Wäa tiedijch oppsteiht, kjemt too waut. [Rempel]
   Who gets up early, amounts to something.
   Wer früh aufsteht, kommt zu was.

574) Wäa vääl aunfangt, dee beendijt weinig. *[Epp]*
   Wäa fäl aunfangt, dee beendijt weinijch. [Rempel]
   Who begins much, that one finishes little.
   Wer viel anfängt, beendet wenig.

575) Wäm Kjoasche jefaule, saul klautre leare.
Who likes cherries, should learn to climb.
Wer Kirschen mag, soll zu klettern erlernen.
* *People must learn the skills to satisfy their own needs.*

576) Wäa een Kopp haft, fählt nich een Hoot. *[Epp]*
Wäa een Kopp haft, fält nijch een Hoot. [Rempel]
Who has a head, lacks not a hat.
Wer einen Kopf hat, fehlt nicht einen Hut.
* *If you have any brains at all, you'll see to providing for basic necessities.*

DE STELLE EM LAUND / THE QUIET ONES IN THE LAND
DIE STILLE IM LANDE

* The Mennonites of Europe were known as the "quiet ones in the land" for their humility, rejection of violence, "yieldedness" to God (Gelassenheit), reserve, restraint, quietude, piety, Christian charity and social separation. While these traits still characterize many Anabaptist communities today, others are now entering politics, missionary work and civic activism with a high degree of public visibility.

577) Stellness un Jedanke kjäne kjeenem krank moake. *[Epp]*
Stellness onn Jedanke kjäne kjeenem krank moake. [Rempel]
Silence and thinking can make no-one sick.
Schweigen und Gedanken kann niemand kränken.

578) Si stomm, wan du jeffst, oba räd, wan maun di jefft! *[Epp]*
Sie stomm, wan dü jefst, oba räd, wan maun die jeft! [Rempel]
Be mute, when you give, but speak, when someone gives to you!
Sei stumm, wenn du gibst, aber sprich, wenn man dir gibt!

579) Si stell, ooda saij waut, daut bäta aus Ruh es! *[Epp]*
Sie stell, ooda saij waut, daut bäta aus Rü es! [Rempel]
Be quiet, or say something, that is better than silence!
Sei still, oder sag was, das besser als Ruhe ist!
* *Be quiet if you don't have anything nice to say.*

580) 'Ne ruhije Tung moakt en kluaka Kopp. *[Epp]*
   Eene rüije Tung moakt een klüaka Kopp. [Rempel]
   A quiet tongue makes a wise head.
   Eine ruhige Zunge macht einen weisen Kopf.

581) Räd weinig, hea vääl. *[Epp]*
   Räd weinijch, hea fäl. [Rempel]
   Speak little, hear much.
   Sprich wenig, höre viel.
   * *Proverbs 18:27 observes that "A truly wise person uses few words."*

582) 'Ne länjre Räd, een kjleena Senn. *[Epp]*
   'Ne lenjre Räd, een kjleena Senn. [Rempel]
   A longer speech, a smaller mind.
   Eine länger Rede, ein kleiner Sinn.

583) De kjleakjsta jefft noh. *[Epp]*
   Dee kjläkjsta jeft no. [Rempel]
   The wisest yields.
   Der klügster gibt nach.

584) Räd es Selwa, Ruh es Gold. *[Epp]*
   Räd es Selwa, Rü es Golt. [Rempel]
   Speech is silver, silence is gold.
   Reden ist Silber, Schweigen ist Gold.

585) Bäta st<u>omm</u> aus d<u>omm</u>.
   Better mute than stupid.
   Besser stumm als dumm.

586) Räd weinig, räd de Woahrheit. *[Epp]*
   Räd weinijch, räd dee Woarheit. [Rempel]
   Speak little, speak the truth.
   Sprich wenig, sprich die Wahrheit.

587) Wäa weinig saigt, brukt weinig too auntwuade. *[Epp]*
   Wäa weinijch saigt, brukt weinijch too auntwuade. [Rempel]
   Who says little, has little to answer for.
   Wer wenig sagt, hat wenig für zu antworten.

588) Met däm Hoot en'e H<u>aund</u>, kjemmt maun gaunz derch daut L<u>aund</u>.
   [Epp]
   Met däm Hoot enn'e H<u>aunt</u>, kjemt maun gaunss derjch daut L<u>aunt</u>.
      [Rempel]
   With the hat in the hand, one comes through the entire land.
   Mit dem Hut in der Hand kommt man durch's ganze Land.

589) Een reinet Muul un 'ne opprechtige Haund,
   dee brinje dän Maun derch jiedet Laund. *[Epp]*
   Een reinet Mül onn 'ne opprejchtijche Haunt,
   dee brinje dän Maun derjch jiedet Launt. [Rempel]
   A clean mouth and honest hand,
   bring the man through every land.
   Ein reines Mund und ehrliche Hand,
   die bringen den Mann durch jedes Land.

590) Kjeene Auntwuat es uk 'ne Auntwuat. *[Epp]*
   Kjeene Auntwuat es uck eene Auntwuat. [Rempel]
   No answer is also an answer.
   Keine Antwort ist auch eine Antwort.

591) Jäwe es bäta aus kjriee.
   To give is better than to receive.
   Geben ist besser als empfangen.

592) Bäta Onraicht too liede aus Onraicht too doone. *[Epp]*
   Bäta Onnrajcht too liede aus Onnrajcht too doone. [Rempel]
   Better to suffer wrong than to do wrong.
   Besser Unrecht zu leiden als Unrecht zu tun.

593) De jlikja Waig es de basta. *[Epp]*
   Dee jlikja Wajch es dee basta. [Rempel]
   The straight way is the best.
   Der gerade Weg ist der beste.

594) Selwst lowe stinkt. *[Epp]*
   Selfst lowe stinkjt. [Rempel]
   Self-praise stinks.
   Selbst loben stinkt.

595) Fräd es de easchte Birjaflicht. *[Epp]*
Fräd es dee easchte Birjaflijcht. [Rempel]
Peace is the citizen's first duty.
Friede ist die erste Bürgerpflicht.

596) Fräd mest't de Felda. *[Epp]*
Fräd mestet dee Felda. [Rempel]
Peace fertilizes the fields.
Friede düngt die Äcker.
Peace brings plenty, wars create famine and ruin.

597) Wäa Kjrigg prädigt, es de Diewel sien Missjoonäa. *[Epp]*
Wäa Kjrijch prädigt, es dee Diewel sien Missjoonäa. [Rempel]
Who preaches war, is the devil's missionary.
Wer Krieg predigt, ist des Teufels Missionar.

598) Aun Gottes Säajen,
Es aules jeläaje.
Upon God's blessings,
Is everything laid.
An Gottes Segen,
Ist alles gelegen.
* Nothing is possible without God's blessings. Pride in human achievement is
* foolish and conceited.*

599) Jlekjlicha es dee, dee toofräd es. *[Epp]*
Jlekjlijcha es dee, dee toofräd es. [Rempel]
Happier is he, who is satisfied.
Glücklicher ist der, der zufrieden ist.

600) Een Jewäah es soogoa een Fiend too sien Eajendäma. *[Epp]*
Een Jewäa es soogoa een Fient too sien Äjendeema. [Rempel]
A weapon is an enemy even to its owner.
Eine Waffe ist sogar ein Feind zu seinem Eigentümer.
* A concrete hazard in the wrong hands, but also a temptation to do evil.

601) Lot daut Peat om Politikj sorje, sien Kopp es jrata. *[Epp]*
Lot daut Peat omm Politikj sorje, sien Kopp es jrata. [Rempel]
Let the horse worry about politics, his head is bigger.
Lass das Pferd um Politik sorgen, sein Kopf ist grösser.

Mennonites in Russia ran their own affairs but avoided politics as "worldly."

602) Schmocke Kjoakje, weinja Heilja.
Fancy churches, few saints.
Elegante Kirchen, weniger Heilige.
Many early Mennonite settlers worshipped in homes; when churches were built they lacked steeples and were generally plain in their décor.

603) 'Ne Duuw sull nich met Krauje fleaje. *[Epp]*
Eene Düw sull nijch met Krauje fläje. [Rempel]
A dove should not fly with crows.
Eine Taube sollte nicht mit Krähen fliegen.
* *A Christian person should avoid keeping corrupt company.*

OABEIT / WORK / ARBEIT

604) De Oabeit lowt dän Woakjmaun. *[Epp]*
Dee Oabeit lowt dän Woakjmaun. [Rempel]
The work praises the workman.
Die Arbeit lobt den Werkmann.
* *The quality of the product reflects the skill and attentiveness of the person who produced it. It can reflect well or poorly.*

605) Aus de Meista, soo daut Woakj. *[Epp]*
Aus dee Meista, soo daut Woakj. [Rempel]
As the master [craftsman], so the work.
Wie der Meister, so das Werk.

606) Dee waut too doone habe, habe kjeene Tiet fe' Trone.
Those who have something to do, have no time for tears.
Die was zu tun haben, haben keine Zeit für Tränen.

607) Eascht de Oabiet, dan daut Spell, noh de Reis kjemmt daut Ziel. *[E.]*
Eascht dee Oabeit, dan daut Spell, no dee Reis kjemt daut Ssiel. [R.]
First the work, then the play, after the journey comes the goal.
Erst die Arbeit, dann das Spiel, nach die Reise kommt das Ziel.

608) Eascht de Oabeit, dan daut Vejneaje. *[Epp]*
Eascht dee Oabeit, dan daut Fejnäje. [Rempel]

First the work, then the pleasure.
Erst die Arbeit, dann das Vergnügen.

609) Draikjje Oabeit, reinet Jeld. *[Epp]*
Drakjje Oabeit, reinet Jelt. [Rempel]
Dirty work, clean money.
Schmutzige Arbeit, reines Geld.
   * *Even if the work involves getting dirty, the money is still just as clean. Another*
   interpretation asserts that work which involves getting your hands dirty
   generates "cleaner" or purer money— that earned by honest toil.

610) Wan du et aul moake mottst,
   kaunst du et dan uk fuats raicht moake. *[Epp]*
Wan dü et aul moake mottst,
kaunst dü et dan uck fuats rajcht moake. [Rempel]
If you already have to do it, then you can also do it just right.
Wenn du es schon machen musst, kannst du es dann auch gleich richtig
machen.

611) Ohne Fliet, ohne Pries. *[Alt.]* Ohne Fliet, ohne Weat. *[Epp]*
One Fliet, one Priess. [Alt.] One Fliet, one Weat. [Rempel]
Without diligence, without value.
Ohne Fleiss, ohne Preis.

612) Sikj rekje, bringt Sääjen.
Loosely: To get yourself moving [working], brings blessing.
Sich regen, bringt Segen.

613) Nemm nich too vääl Hei opp diene Forkj! *[Epp]*
Nem nijch too fäl Hei opp diene Forkj! [Rempel]
Do not take too much hay on your fork!
Nimm nicht zu viel Heu auf deiner Heugabel!
   * *Don't take on more responsibility or work than you can handle.*

614) Een schlaichta Woakjmaun schellt siene Jeräte. *[Epp]*
Een schlajchta Woakjmaun schellt siene Jerätschoft. [Rempel]
A bad workman blames his tools.
Ein schlechter Werkmann beschuldigt seine Werkzeuge.

615) Ohne Oabeit jefft et kjeen Broot. *[Epp]*

One Oabeit jeft et kjeen Broot. [Rempel]
Without work there is no bread.
Ohne Arbeit gibt es kein Brot.

616) Aus de Oabeit, soo daut Loohn. *[Epp]*
      Aus dee Oabeit, soo daut Loon [Rempel]
      As the work, so the reward.
      Wie die Arbeit, so der Lohn.

Twee Schlätels.

617) Daut Enj kjreent daut Woakj.
      The end (result) crowns the work.
      Das Ende krönt das Werk.

618) Oabeit un ät, ooda si hungrig. *[Epp]*
      Oabeit onn ät, ooda sie hungrijch. [Rempel]
      Work and eat, or be hungry.
      Arbeit und ess, oder sei hungrig.

619) Mässigkjeit haft Oarmoot fe' Leehna. *[Epp]*
      Mässijchkjeit haft Oarmoot fe' Leena. [Rempel]
      Idleness has poverty for wages.
      Untätigkeit hat Armut für Löhne.

620) De Diewel fingt Oabeit fe' mässje Hänj too doone. *[Epp]*
      Dee Diewel fingt Oabeit fe' mässje Henj too doone. [Rempel]

The devil finds work for idle hands to do.
Der Teufel findet Arbeit für untätige Hände zu tun.
* Those who keep busy at work have less time and energy for sinful behavior.

621) Een jebrukta Pluag blenkjat, oba stohnendet Wota stinkjt. *[Epp]*
Een jebruckta Plüach blenkjat, oba stonendet Wota stinkjt. [Rempel]
A used plow shines, standing water stinks.
Ein benutzter Pflug glänzt, aber stehender Wasser stinkt.
* An idle person is like the standing water.

622) Weinja Rot un mea Hänj. *[Epp]*
Weinja Rot onn mea Henj. [Rempel]
Less advice and more hands.
Weniger Rat und mehr Hände.
* Get to work, and stop theorizing about how to do the job.

623) Schwind wäahrend Moltiet, schwind wäahrend Oabeit. *[Epp]*
Schwind wäarent Moltiet, schwind wäarent Oabeit. [Rempel]
Quick during mealtime, quick during work.
Schnell während Mahlzeit, schnell während Arbeit.

624) Aus de Goadna, soo de Goade. *[Epp]*
Aus dee Goadna, soo dee Goade. [Rempel]
As the gardener, so the gardener.
Als der Gärtner, so der Garten.

625) Selwst jedone es boold jedone. *[Epp]*
Selfst jedone es boolt jedone. [Rempel]
Self-done is soon done.
Selbst getan ist bald getan.
** Do it yourself and it gets done quickly. Wait for others to do it, and you may be
waiting a long time.*

626) 'Ne Fruu äahre Oabeit es niemols foadig. *[Epp]*
Eene Frü äare Oabeit es niemols foadijch. [Rempel]
A woman's work is never done.
Die Arbeit einer Frau ist nie getan.

627) Wua et too vääl Woakjmana jefft, jefft et weinig Oabeit. *[Epp]*
Wua et too fäl Werkjmanna jeft, jeft et weinijch Oabeit. [Rempel]

Where there are too many workmen, there is little work.
Wo es zu viele Arbeiter gibt, gibt es wenig Arbeit.

628) Mät dusendmol, un schnied eenmol. *[Epp]*
Mät düsentmol, onn schnied eenmol. [Rempel]
Measure a thousand times, and cut one time.
Mess tausendmal, und schneid einmal.

629) 'Ne schoape Aix fingt een Steen. *[Epp]*
'Ne schoape Akjs fingt een Steen. [Rempel]
A sharp axe finds a stone.
Eine scharfe Axt findet einen Stein.
* New equipment is often prone to early damage. Pebbles seem to be attracted by
  new windshields, for example.

630) He weet woo de Forkj em Stähl staikt. *[Epp]*
Hee weet woo dee Forkj emm Stähl staikt. [Rempel]
He knows how the pitchfork goes into the handle.
Er weiß wie die Heugabel im Stiel steckt.
* He knows what he's doing.

TRUBBEL / TROUBLE / MÜHE

631) He weet waut ahm jebrode es. *[Epp]*
Hee weet waut am jebrode es. [Rempel]
He knows what is fried for him.
Er weiß was ihm gebraten ist.
* He knows what is in store for him. This may relate to the fact that sometimes
  marginal ingedients are fried to hide their low quality. An early trip to the
  kitchen may leave a person knowing all too well what is fried for him/her.

632) Vondoag root, morje doot. *[Epp]*
Fonndoag root, morje doot. [Rempel]
Today red (rosy-cheeked), tomorrow dead.
Heute rot, morgen tot.

633) Aum Aunfang heet et "läwe lang,"
daut Enj kjlingt et aus Graufjesang. *[Epp]*
Aum Aunfank heet et "läwe lank,"

128

daut Enj kjlingt et aus Graufjes<u>ank</u>. [Rempel]
The beginning of it [a text] reads "live long," the ending clangs like
grave- song [a dirge].
Am Anfang heißt es "lebe lang," das Ende klang wie Grabgesang.

634) Aula Aunfang es schwoa. *[Epp]*
Aula Aunfank es schwoa. [Rempel]
Every beginning is difficult.
Aller Anfang ist schwer.

635) Et jefft nuscht schlemmeret, aus 'ne Fruu ohne een Maun. [Epp]
Et jeft nuscht schlemmeret, aus 'ne Frü one een Maun. [Rempel]
There is nothing worse, than a woman without a man.
Es gibt nichts schlimmeres, als eine Frau ohne einen Mann.

636) En de Nacht schlapt daut Jesatz. *[Epp]*
Enn dee Nacht schlapt daut Jesats. [Rempel]
The law sleeps at night.
Bei Nacht schläft das Gesetz.

637) Wää sikj en Jefoah bejefft, kjemmt en'e Jefoah om. *[Epp]*
Wää sikj enn Jefoa bejeft, kjemt enne Jefoa omm. [Rempel]
Who exposes himself to danger, perishes from danger.
Wer sich in Gefahr begibt, kommt in der Gefahr um.

638) De Schraikj haft groote Uage. *[Epp]*
Dee Schrakj haft groote Üage. [Rempel]
Terror has big eyes.
Der Schreck hat große Augen.

639) De Fercht haft dusend Uage. *[Epp]*
Dee Ferjcht haft düsent Üage. [Rempel]
Fear has a thousand eyes.
Der Furcht hat tausand Augen.

640) Fercht moakt Aufgottsdeenst. *[Epp]*
Ferjcht moakt Aufgottsdeenst. [Rempel]
Fear makes idolatry.
Furcht macht Götzendienst.

129

641) Metjegohne, metjefonge, metjehonge. *[Epp]*
Metjegone, metjefonge, metjehonge. [Rempel]
Gone with, caught with, hung with.
Mitgegangen, mitgefangen, mitgehangen.
* Associate with the wrong crowd, and they will bring you down.

642) Schietaja Wausch un Schulde saumle sikj haustig. *[Epp]*
Schietaja Wausch onn Schulde saumle sikj haustijch. [Rempel]
Shitty laundry and debt accumulate themselves quickly.
Scheissigen Wäsche und Schulden sammeln sich rasch.

643) Oolet Fiendschoft es boold wada nie jemoakt. *[Epp]*
Oolet Fientschoft es boolt wada nie jemoakt. [Rempel]
Old enmity is soon made new again.
Alte Feindschaft ist bald erneuert.

644) Mea Fiende, mea Eah. *[Epp]*
Mea Fiende, mea Ea. [Rempel]
More enemies, more honor.
Mehr Feinde, mehr Ehre.

645) Daut dikje Enj kjemmt noh. *[Epp]*
Daut dikje Enj kjemt no. [Rempel]
The thick end [of the switch] is still coming.
Das dicke Ende kommt nach.
* It is going to get worse before it gets better.

646) De Mensche send nich emma waut se schiene. *[Epp]*
Dee Mensche send nijch emma waut see schiene. [Rempel]
People are not always what they appear.
Leute sind nicht immer, was sie scheinen.

647) Lied ändre foaken, un selde toom bätre. *[Epp]*
Lied endre foake, onn selde toom bätre. [Rempel]
People change often, and seldon for the better.
Leute ändern häufig, und selten zum besseren.

648) He wea mi en Stachel em Uag. *[Epp]*
Hee wea mie een Stachel emm Üag. [Rempel]
He was a thorn in my eye.

Er war mir ein Dorn im Auge.

649) De Dood jefft kjeene Auntwuat. *[Epp]*
Dee Doot jeft kjeene Auntwuat. [Rempel]
Death gives no answer.
Der Tod gibt keine Antwort.

650) Dee send nich aula Kochasch, dee lange Massasch droage. *[Epp]*
Dee send nijch aule Kochasch, dee lange Massasch droage. [Rempel]
They are not all cooks, that carry long knives.
Die sind nicht alle Köche, die lange Messers tragen.
  * *This saying is likely of Russian/Ukrainian origin, but when it "crossed over"*
    into Plautdietsch will never be known.

651) Wää de Schode haft, dee woat dän Spott uk kjriee. *[Epp]*
Wää dee Schode haft, dee woat dän Spott uck kjrieje. [Rempel]
Who has tribulations, that one will also get mockery.
Wer der Schaden hat, der wird auch den Spott bekommen.

652) De vedrinkjendja Maun hält aun Strooh fast. *[Epp]*
Dee fedrinkjendja Maun hällt aun Stroo faust. [Rempel]
The drowning man grabs at straw.
Der ertrinkende Mann ergreift Stroh.

653) Wan de Himmel fällt, woare wi de Leewoakje fange. *[Epp]*
Wan dee Himmel fällt, woare wie dee Leewoakje fange. [Rempel]
If the sky falls, we will catch the larks.
Wenn der Himmel fällt, werden wir die Lerchen fangen.
  * *Even faced with the gravest trouble, one can find some advantage or survival*
    strategy. This is the resilience of a people repeatedly uprooted and persecuted.

654) Diewels wohne en stelle Wotalaicha. *[Epp]*
Diewels wone enn stelle Wotalajcha. [Rempel]
Devils live in peaceful ponds.
Teufel bewohnen ruhige Teiche.
  * *Look for trouble in unexpected places and faces that seem safe. A Russian*
    version warns that "В тихом о́муте че́рти во́дятся--" [V tikhom omute cherti
    vodyatsa.] "Still waters are inhabited by devils."

655) Mea Lied vedrinkje en en Wienglaus aus em Mäa. *[Epp]*
Mea Lied fedrinkje enn een Wienglauss aus emm Mäa. [Rempel]

131

More people drown in a wineglass than in the sea.
Mehr Leute ertrinken in einem Weinglass als im Meer.

656) Et es bäta kjeen Dokta too habe aus dree.
   It is better to have no doctor than to have three.
   Es ist besser keinen Arzt zu haben als drei.
   * *It is better because three doctors together can mismanage a case; also, if you*
   have three doctors you may be quite ill, but if you have no doctor the chances
   are that your health is good.

657) Een junga Dokta velangt en niea Frädhoff. *[Epp]*
   Een junga Dokta felangt een nie Frädhoff. [Rempel]
   A young doctor requires a new cemetery.
   Ein junger Arzt verlangt einen neuen Kirchhof.
   * *This is because of the fatal mistakes he'll make until he gets experience.*

658) Een bätje lot es vääl too lot. *[Epp]*
   Een bätje lot es fäl too lot. [Rempel]
   A little bit late is much too late.
   Ein bisschen spät ist viel zu spät.

659) Wan een Deef di kusst, tall diene Tähne. *[Epp]*
   Wan een Deef die kusst, tall diene Täne. [Rempel]
   When a thief kisses you, count your teeth.
   Wenn ein Dieb dich küßt, zähl deine Zähne.

660) Met soone Frind bruckt maun kjeene Fiend mea.
   With such friends one needs no more enemies.
   Mit solchen Freunden braucht man keine Feinde mehr.

661) De Mala es eahlich, dee Hoa opp siene Tähne haft. [Epp]
   Dee Mala es ealijch, dee Hoa opp siene Täne haft. [Rempel]
   The miller is honest, who has hair on his teeth.
   Der Müller ist ehrlich, der Haar auf seinen Zähnen hat.
   * *Millers often amassed more wealth than the farmers who relied on them, and*
   were often suspected of dishonesty.

662) Too jiede Auntwuat kaun eena niea Froage finje.
   To every answer one can find new questions.
   Zu jeder Antwort kann man neue Fragen finden.

663) Jlekj un Onjlekj send twee Amasch en een Borm. *[Epp]*
Jlekj onn Onnjlekj send twee Amasch enn een Borm. [Rempel]
Fortune and misfortune are two buckets in a well.
Glück und Unglück sind zwei Eimers in einem Brunnen.
   * *Life is just as likely to bring misery as it is happiness, and both can come from*
     the same source.

664) Nuscht es niemols en Jefoah. *[Epp]*
Nuscht es niemols enn Jefoa. [Rempel]
Nothing is never in danger.
Nichts ist nie in die Gefahr.
   * *Everything is always at risk at some point. If someone promises something risk-*
     free, think twice.

665) Pacht un Taxe schlope nich. *[Epp]*
Pacht onn Tackse schlope nijch. [Rempel]
Rent and taxes don't sleep.
Miete und Steuern schlafen nicht.

666) Een ladja Buck, een schwoaret Hoat.
An empty belly, a heavy heart.
Ein leerer Bauch, ein schweres Herz.

667) Loagre mang Deew, oppwakje met Oarme.
Bed down among thieves, awaken with paupers.
Lagern mitten Diebe, aufwecken mit Arme.

668) Ordninj rejeat de Welt, un een Kjneppel de Mensche. *[Epp]*
Ordninj rejeat dee Weld, onn een Kjneppel dee Mensche. [Rempel]
Order governs the world, and a cudgel the people.
Ordnung regiert die Welt, und ein Knüppel die Menschen.

HUUS UN HEIM / HOUSE AND HOME / HAUS UND HEIM

669) Froag noh de Nobasch, kjeep dan daut Huus. *[Epp]*
Froag no dee Nobasch, kjeep dan daut Hüss. [Rempel]
Ask about the neighbors, then you buy the house.

Frag nach den Nachbarn, kauf dann das Haus.

670) Em Ooste un Waste, t'huus es et baste. *[Epp]*
Emm Ooste onn Waste, Tüss es et baste. [Rempel]
In the east and the west, at home it is best.
Im Osten und Westen, zu Hause ist beste.

671) Ekj si noch emma Har en mien Huus;
Ekj kaun doch sette wua ekj well. *[Epp]*
Ekj sie noch emma Har enn mien Hüss;
Ekj kaun doch sette wua ekj well. [Rempel]
I am still lord in my house; I can still sit where I want.
Ich bin noch immer Herr in mein Haus;
Ich kann doch sitzen wo ich will.

Dit Huus wea em Joah 1915 jebuut. [author]

672) Jieda es Kjeisa en sien eajnet Huus. *[Epp]*
Jieda es Kjeisa enn sien äjnet Hüss. [Rempel]
Everyone is emperor in his own house.
Jeder ist Kaiser in seinem eigenen Haus.

673) De Oarma es een Kjeenig t'huus. *[Epp]*
Dee Oarma es een Kjeenijch Tüss. [Rempel]
The poor man is a king at home.
Der Arme ist ein König zu Hause.

674) De Oarma buut een kjleenet Huus. *[Epp]*
Dee Oarma büt een kjleenet Hüss. [Rempel]
The poor one builds a small house.
Der Arme baut ein kleines Haus.

675) Wan daut Huus foadig es, dan kjemmt dän Dood. *[Epp]*
Wan daut Hüss foadijch es, dan kjemt dän Doot. [Rempel]
When the house is finished, then comes death.
Wann das Haus fertig ist, kommt dann den Tod.
  * *This echoes a famous Swabian rhyme, "Schaffe, spare, Häusle Baue..." Work, save, build your little house..." Then you die.*

676) Bi mi t'huus si ekj de Meista. *[Epp]*
Bie mie Tüss sie ekj dee Meista. [Rempel]
With me at home I am master.
Bei mir zu Haus bin ich der Herr.

Dit aundret Huus es sea groot un fein. [author]

677) Kjikj eascht en dien Huus, dan kjikj 'erut. *[Epp]*
Kjikj eascht enn dien Hüss, dan kjikj erüt. [Rempel]
First look in your house, then look outside!
Sieh erst in dein Haus, dann sieh heraus!
  * *Examine yourself and your household before you scrutinize or judge others.*

678) De jratsta Schrett es uut de Däa. *[Epp]*
Dee jratsta Schrett es üt dee Däa. [Rempel]
The biggest step is out the door.

Der größste Schritt ist aus der Tür.
* Leave home and you enter the unknown.

679) Eajnet H<u>ea</u>d es Gold sien W<u>ea</u>t. *[Epp]*
Äjnet H<u>ea</u>t es Golt sien W<u>ea</u>t. [Rempel]
Your own hearth is worth gold.
Eigner Herd ist Goldes wert.

680) Too Gaust es goot, mau t'huus es bäta. *[Epp]*
Too Gaust es goot, mau Tüss es bäta. [Rempel]
To [be] a guest is good, but at home is better.
Es ist gut, ein Gast zu sein, aber zu Hause ist besser.

681) Met vääl hällt maun Huus, met weinig kjemmt maun uut. *[Epp]*
Met fäl hällt maun Hüss, met weinijch kjemt maun üt. [Rempel]
With much one keeps house, with little one comes out.
Mit vielen hält man Haus, mit wenig kommt man aus.

682) 'Ne rikje Fruu em Huus lascht de Fräd uut. *[Epp]*
Eene rikje Frü emm Hüss lascht dee Fräd üt. [Rempel]
A rich woman in the house drives the peace out.
Eine reiche Frau im Haus treibt den Frieden aus.

683) Kjeen Huus ohne 'ne Muus. *[Epp]*
Kjeen H<u>üs</u>s one eene M<u>üs</u>s. [Rempel]
No house without a mouse.
Kein Haus ohne eine Maus.
No person or thing is free from pests, flaws and problems.

684) Et es daut bastet Feld, maun sien eajnet es. *[Epp]*
Et es daut bastet Felt, maun sien äjnet es. [Rempel]
It is the best field, that is one's own.
Das ist der beste Acker, der man sein eigener ist.

AUNDRE SAIJE / OTHER SAYINGS / ANDERE REDENSARTEN

685) Met een Deef fangt maun Deew.
With a thief one catches thieves.

Mit ein Dieb fangt man Diebe.

686) Wäa eenmol stählt, es emma een Deef. *[Epp]*
    Wäa eenmol stält, es emma een Deef. [Rempel]
    Who steals once, is always a thief.
    Wer einmal stiehlt, ist immer ein Dieb.

687) Du best een Enjel met en "B" doaväa. *[Epp]*
    Du best een Enjel met een "B" doafäa. [Rempel]
    [Lit.] You are an angel with a "B" in front of it.
    Du bist ein Engel mit ein "B" davor.
    * A Benjel (PD) or Bengel (Ger.) is a "rascal," no angel at all!

688) Kjleen, oba mient.
    Small, but mine.
    Klein, aber mein.

689) Maun saul dän Dag nich ver'em Owend lowe. *[Epp]*
    Maun saul dän Dach nijch fer däm Owent lowe. [Rempel]
    One should not praise the day before the evening.
    Man soll den Tag nicht vor dem Abend loben.

690) Wua et mi goot jeiht, doa es mien Vodalaund. *[Epp]*
    Wua et mie goot jeit, doa es mien Fodalaunt. [Rempel]
    Where it goes well for me, there is my fatherland.
    Wo mir's gut geht, ist mein Vaterland.

691) Grootet Muul, kjleenet Jehirn. *[Epp]*
    Grootet Mül, kjleenet Jehirn. [Rempel]
    Big mouth, small brain.
    Großes Mund, kleines Gehirn.

692) Soo jenauw scheete de Preisse nich. *[Epp]*
    Soo jeneiw scheete dee Preisse nijch. [Rempel]
    The Prussians don't shoot so accurately.
    So genau schiessen die Preussen nicht.
    * Perhaps this is an echo of the Prussian intolerance that caused Mennonites to
      leave the Danzig area for Russia. Prussians were unpopular for their aggressive,
      militant behavior and even today Germans may call a rigid authoritarian person
      a "Preuss." One might also read this as "experts don't always perform well."
      The Prussians were the expert soldiers of central Europe.

693) Waut maun haft, daut haft maun.
What one has, that [is what] one has.
Was man hat, das hat man.

694) Meddelmässigkjeit es goot un fein,
bloos doawst du nich onmässig senne. *[Epp]*
Meddelmässijchkjeit es goot onn fein,
blooss doawst dü nijch onnmässijch senne. [Rempel]
Moderation is good and fine, just don't you be immoderate [about it].
Mässigkeit ist gut und fein, aber darfst du nicht unmässig sein.

695) Niea Wien en oole Buddle. *[Epp]*
Niea Wien enn oole Buddle. [Rempel]
New wine in old bottles.
Neuer Wein in alten Flaschen.
* *Something of low quality being passed off as a better product-- a swindle.*

696) Kjeena kaun et aule Lied raicht moake. *[Epp]*
Kjeena kaun et aule Lied rajcht moake. [Rempel]
Nobody can do it right for all the people.
Keiner kann es alle Leute recht machen.

697) Ordnung rejeat de Welt, oba de Mensche brucke de
Wipp [alt. dän Kjneppel]. *[Epp]*
Ordninj rejeat dee Welt, oba dee Mensche brucke dee
Wipp [alt. dän Kjneppel]. [Rempel]
Order rules the world, but people need the whip [alt. club].
Ordnung regiert die Welt, aber die Menschen brauchen der
Peitsche [alt. den Knüppel].

698) Sejcha es sejcha.
Sure is sure.
Sicher ist sicher.

699) Wies mi diene Frind, un ekj saij di wäa du best. *[Epp]*
Wies mie diene Frind, onn ekj saij die wäa dü best. [Rempel]
Show me your friends and I tell you who you are.
Zeige mir deine Freunde, und ich sage dir wer du bist.

700) Bloot es dikja aus Wota.
Blood is thicker than water.
Blut ist dicker als Wasser.

701) Kjleene Schmauntkaune habe uk Uahre. *[Epp]*
Kjleene Schmauntkaune habe uck Uare. [Rempel]
Little cream-cans also have ears.
Kleine Sahnekrüge haben auch Ohren.
* Watch what you say around small children.*

702) Met wäm maun omjeiht, daut hängt eenem aun. *[Epp]*
Met wäm maun ommjeit, daut hängt eenem aun. [Rempel]
Who one goes around with, that hangs on one.
Mit wem man umgeht, das hängt man an.

703) Korte Enja send nich lenja. *[Epp]*
Korte Enja send nijch lenja. [Rempel]
Short ends are not longer.
Kurze Ende sind nicht länger.

704) Nohm lache kjemmt hiele. *[Epp]*
Nom lache kjemt hiele. [Rempel]
After laughing comes crying.
Nach lachen kommt weinen.

705) Et es bloos 'ne Drepp opp en heeta Steen. *[Epp]*
Et es blooss 'ne Drepp opp een' heeta Steen. [Rempel]
It is only a drop on a hot stone.
Es ist nur ein Tropfen auf einem heißen Stein.

706) Daut Iesa es schmiedig, soo lang et heet es. *[Epp]*
Daut Iesa es schmiedijch, soo lang et heet es. [Rempel]
The iron is pliable, as long as it is hot.
Das Eisen ist geschmiedig, wie lang es heiß ist.

707) Eent "ekj hab" es bäta aus tieen "ekj haud." *[Epp]*
Eent "ekj hab" es bäta aus tian "ekj haud." [Rempel]
One "I have" is better than ten "I had."
Ein "ich habe" ist besser als zehn "ich hatte."

708) Wan de Wien en es, dan es de Kluakheit uut. *[Epp]*
    Wan dee Wien enn es , dan es de Klüakheit üt. [Rempel]
    When the wine is in, the wisdom is out.
    Wann der Wein in ist, dann ist die Weisheit aus.

709) Maun un W<u>ief</u> send een <u>Lief</u>. *[Epp]*
    Maun onn W<u>ief</u> send een L<u>ief</u>. [Rempel]
    Man and wife are one body.
    Mann und Weib sind ein Leib.

710) Een volla Buck studeat nich jearn. *[Epp]*
    Een folla Buck studeat nijch jearn. [Rempel]
    A full belly prefers not to study.
    Ein voller Bauch studiert nicht gern.

711) Bäta tweemol mäte, aus eenmol vejäte. *[Epp]*
    Bäta tweemol <u>mäte</u>, aus eenmol fej<u>äte</u>. [Rempel]
    Better to measure twice, than forget once.
    Besser zweimal messen, als einmal vergessen.

712) Kjeene Weissheit, kjeen Vestaund,
    Kjeen Rot besteiht ver'em Har. *[Epp]*
    Kjeene Weissheit, kjeen Festaunt,
    Kjeen Rot besteiht fer däm Har. [Rempel]
    No wisdom, no understanding,
    No counsel exists before the Lord.
    Keine Weisheit, kein Verstand,
    Kein Rat besteht vor dem Herrn.

713) Waut boold riep woat, woat boold fuul. *[Epp]*
    Waut boolt riep es, woat boolt fül. [Rempel]
    What soon ripens is soon rotten.
    Was bald reif wird, wird bald faul.

714) Sorj nich wan du bäde kaunst. *[Epp]*
    Sorj nijch wan dü bäde kaunst. [Rempel]
    Don't worry when you can pray.
    Sorg nicht wenn du beten kannst.

715) Et jeiht aules vebi. *[Epp]*
Et jeit aules febie. [Rempel]
Everything shall pass.
Es geht alles vorbei.

716) Et jefft kjeen Weit ohne Sprie. *[Epp]*
Et jeft kjeen Weit one Sprie. [Rempel]
There is no wheat without chaff.
Es gibt kein Weizen ohne Spreu.

717) Gooda Nohrecht moakt stoakje Been. *[Epp]*
Gooda Norejcht moakt stoakje Been. [Rempel]
Good news makes strong legs.
Gute Nachricht macht starke Beine.

718) Eenmol es kjeenmol.
One time is never.
Einmal ist keinmal.

719) Bäta lot aus niemols.
Better late than never.
Besser spät als nie.

720) Freid un Sorj send Nobasch. *[Epp]*
Freid onn Sorj send Nobasch. [Rempel]
Joy and sorrow are neighbors.
Freude und Sorge sind Nachbarn.

721) Toofrädenheit es de jratsta Rikjdoom. *[Epp]*
Toofrädenheit es dee jratsta Rikjdom. [Rempel]
Contentment is the greatest wealth.
Zufriedenheit ist der größte Reichtum.

722) De Jesunde un de Kranke habe Jedanke dee nich äwareen send. *[Epp]*
Dee Jesunte onn dee Kranke habe Jedanke dee nijch äwareen
send. [Rempel]
The healthy and the sick have different thoughts.
Die Gesunden und die Kranken haben unähnliche Gedanke.

723) Maun kaun uk met Papia morde. *[Epp]*
Maun kaun uck met Papia morde. [Rempel]
One can also murder with paper.
Mann kann auch mit Papier morden.

724) Je jel<u>ea</u>da, je vekj<u>ea</u>da. *[Epp]*
Je leleada, je fekjeada. [Rempel]
The more learned, the more wrong.
Je gelehrte, desto verkehrte.
Rural Mennonites sometimes distrusted formal learning, favoring common
experience as a better guide. However, Russian Mennonites founded excellent
schools both in Europe and the New World, and today the Kansas college with the
highest academic rating is Bethel College-- a Mennonite institution.

725) Waut du kaunst vondoag bes<u>orj</u>e,
daut schuuw nich opp bott M<u>orj</u>e. *[Epp]*
Waut dü kaunst fonndoag bes<u>orj</u>e,
daut schuuw nijch opp bott M<u>orj</u>e. [Rempel]
What you can take care of today, that do not put off until tomorrow.
Was du heute kannst besorgen, das verzögert nicht bis morgen.

726) De Väaschien vedreiht. *[Epp]*
Dee Fäaschien fedreit. [Rempel]
Appearance distorts.
Der Anschein verzerrt.

727) Eene Haund wauscht de aundre. *[Epp]*
Eene Haunt wauscht dee aundre. [Rempel]
One hand washes the other.
Eine Hand wäscht die andere.

728) Leah too jeheare, om too befähle. *[Epp]*
Lea too jeheare, omm too befäle. [Rempel]
Learn to obey, in order to command.
Lern zu befolgen, zwecks zu befehlen.

729) De jlikja Waig es de baste. *[Epp]*
Dee jlikja Wajch es dee baste. [Rempel]
The straight way is the best.
Der gerade Weg ist der beste.

730) Nu es miene Moht voll. *[Epp]*
Nu es miene Mot foll. [Rempel]
Now my measure is full.
Nun ist mein Maß voll.
* Now I'm totally fed-up.

731) Pinktlichkjeit es de Heeflichkjeit von de Groote. *[Epp]*
Pinkjlijchkjeit es dee Heeflijchkjeit fonn dee Groote. [Rempel]
Punctuality is the courtesy of the great.
Pünktlichkeit ist die Höflichkeit der Großen.

732) Bi de Menniste jefft et vääl bunte Hunj dee "Mopps" heete. *[Epp]*
Bie dee Menniste jeft et fäl bunte Hunj dee "Mopps" heete. [R.]
Among the Mennonites there are many colorful dogs named "Mopps."
Bei dän Mennonieten gibt es viele bunte Hünde die Mopps heissen.
* "Mopps" means "chubby." This saying expresses "familial" similarity that
Mennonites find when visiting separated enclaves. The names, values,
behavior, and often physical appearances remind the people of home.

733) Seete Weada kjenne een schlemmet Hoat vestäakje. *[Epp]*
Seete Wead kjenne een schlemmet Hoat festäakje. [Rempel]
Sweet words can hide a wicked heart.
Süße Wörter können ein schlechtes Herz verstecken.

734) Dank kost't nuscht un doch jefällt Gott un Mensche goot. *[Epp]*
Dank kostet nuscht onn doch jefällt Gott onn Mensche goot. [R.]
Thanks cost nothing and yet pleases God and man well.
Dank kostet nichts und doch gefällt Gott und Menschen wohl.

735) Kjinja froage met Zocka bestreit. *[Epp]*
Kjinja froage met Ssocka bestreit. [Rempel]
Children ask [questions] strewn with sugar.
Kinder fragen mit Zucker bestreut.
* The questions of children are sweet because of their innocence.

736) Erre es menschlich; vejäwe es gottesähnlich. *[Epp]*
Erre es menschlijch; fejäwe es gottesänlijch. [Rempel]
To err is human; to forgive is god-like.
Irren ist menschlich; verzeihen ist gottähnlich.

737) Waut ekj nich weet, moakt mi nich heet. *[Epp]*
Waut ekj nijch w<u>eet</u>, moakt mie nijch h<u>eet</u>. *[Rempel]*
What I don't know, doesn't make me hot [angry].
Was ich nicht weiß, macht mir nicht heiß.

738) Uut nuscht woat nuscht. *[Epp]*
Üt nuscht woat nuscht. *[Rempel]*
From nothing comes nothing.
Aus nichts wird nichts.

739) Doo waut du kaunst, met waut du hast, wua du best! *[Epp]*
Doo waut dü kaunst, met waut dü hast, wua dü best! *[Rempel]*
Do what you can, with what you have, where you are!
Tu was du kannst, mit was du hast, wo du bist!

740) Jieda es de Schmett von sien eajnet Jlekj. *[Epp]*
Jieda es dee Schmett fonn sien äjnet Jlekj. *[Rempel]*
Everyone is the blacksmith of his fortune.
Jeder ist der Schmied seines Vermögens.

741) Een Mensch hopt soo lang he läwt. *[Epp]*
Een Mensch hopt soo lang hee läwt. *[Rempel]*
A person hopes as long as he lives.
Ein Mensch hofft so lange er lebt.

742) Aule goode Dinja send dree.
All good things are three.
Alle gute Dinge sind drei.

743) Vejäwe es leichta aus vejäte. *[Epp]*
Fejäwe es leijchta aus fejäte. *[Rempel]*
To forgive is easier than to forget.
Verzeihen ist einfacher als vergessen.

744) Vääl Doagesoabeit, weinja Nachtjeschwien. *[Epp]*
Fäl Doagesoabeit, weinja Nachtjeschwien. *[Rempel]*
Much work by day, less nocturnal misbehavior.
Viel Tagesarbeit, weniger Nachtschweinerei.

745) Jiedet Krulkje haft een Dulkje.
   Every little lock has a little devil.
   Jedes Löckchen hat ein Teufelchen.
   * Stylish hair can attract romantic attention and also be a source of personal
   vanity.

746) Bäta en kjleena Har aus een groota Kjnaicht. *[Epp]*
   Bäta een kjleena Har aus een groota Kjnajcht. [Rempel]
   Better a small master [lord] than a big servant.
   Besser ein kleiner Herr als ein großer Knecht.

747) Niee Bassems fäaje goot.
   New brooms sweep well.
   Neue Besen fegen gut.

748) Beschutz diene Eah aum längste. *[Epp]*
   Beschuts diene Ea aum lengste. [Rempel]
   Protect your honor the longest.
   Beschütz deine Ehre am längste.

749) De Dood kjant kjeen Jesatz,
   he nemmt dän Kjeenig jrod soo aus de Oarme. *[Epp]*
   Dee Doot kjant kjeen Jesats,
   hee nemt dän Kjeenijch jrod soo aus dee Oarme. [Rempel]
   Death recognizes no law, he takes the king just like the pauper.
   Der Tod kennt kein Gesetz, er nimmt den König wie auch den Armen.

750) Schmet frat aulawäajens met, Leewe wull daut nich jleewe,
   Friese wull daut bewiese, oba de Dohle motte betohle. *[Epp]*
   Schmet frat aulawääje met, Leewe wull daut nijch jleewe,
   Friese wull daut bewiese, oba dee Dohle motte betole. [Rempel]
   Schmidt gorged everywhere, Loewen wanted not to beliewe it,
   Friesen wanted to prove it, but the Dahl's must pay for it.
   Schmidt frisst überall mit, Löwen will das nicht glauben,
   Friesen will das erweisen, aber die Dahlen müssen bezahlen.
   * These are all typical German-Russian Mennonite surnames. They are usually
   written the conventional German way, but traditionally pronounced as the
   Plautdietsch spellings indicate. Thus a name like "Toews" rhymes with the
   English word "shaves," which might surprise a reader familiar with only High
   German. Similarly, the name "Thiessen" rhymes with "Lisa," the ending "n"
   being absent like the ending "n" on Plautdietsch verb infinitives.

751) Kjeene Rääjle ohne Utnohme. *[Epp]*
Kjeene Rääjle one Ütnome. [Rempel]
No rules without exceptions.
Keine Regeln ohne Ausnahmen.

752) Strenje Hares rejiere nich lang. *[Epp]*
Strenje Haress rejiare nijch lang. [Rempel]
Strict masters [lords] do not rule long.
Strenge Herren regieren nicht lang.

753) Jiede Sach haft twee Siede, miene Sied es de raichte. *[Epp]*
Jiede Sach haft twee Siede, miene Sied es dee rajchte. [Rempel]
Every issue has two sides, mine is the right [one].
Jede Sache hat zwei Seiten, meine Seite ist die richtige.
  * When a parent made this statement to argumentative or petitioning teens, it
    signaled that the debate was over, according to the source of this saying.

754) Frind hinja däm Rigje send aus stoakje Brigje.
Friends behind the back are like strong bridges.
Freunde hinter dem Rücken sind wie starke Brücken.

755) Es de Kopp aufjeschnäde, woat kjeena noh däm Hoot froage. *[Epp]*
Es dee Kopp aufjeschnäde, woat kjeena no däm Hoot froage. [R.]
[If] the head was cut off, no one will ask about the hat.
Ist der Kopf abgeschitten, wird niemand nach dem Hut fragen.

756) Wan "wan" nich wea, wea Koohschiet Zockamezpaun. *[Epp]*
Wan "wan" nijch wea, wea Kooschiet Ssocka met Spon. [Rempel]
If "if" were not if, then cowshit would be sugar candy.
Wenn "wenn" nicht war, war Kuhscheiss Marzipan.

757) Eajne Laust es nich schwoa. *[Epp]*
Äjne Laust es nijch schwoa. [Rempel]
Your own burden is not heavy.
Eigene Last ist nicht schwer.

758) De Äsel jefft sien Rot fe' nuscht. *[Epp]*
Dee Äsel jeft sien Rot fe' nuscht. [Rempel]
The jackass gives his advice for nothing.

Der Esel gibt sein Rat für nichts.

759) Eascht de Oabeit, dan daut Schmenje. *[Epp]*
     Eascht dee Oabeit, dan daut Schmenje. [Rempel]
     First the work, than the tasting.
     Erst die Arbeit, dann das Kosten.

760) Noch es dee Mensch nich jebuare,
     dee et fe' aule Lied raicht moake kaun. *[Epp]*
     Noch es dee Mensch nijch jebuare,
     dee et fe' aule Lied rajcht moake kaun. [Rempel]
     He is still not born, who can make it right for all people.
     Noch ist der Mensch nicht geboren,
     der es für alle Leute recht machen kann.

761) Maun kaun nich met däm Kopp derch 'ne Waund gohne. *[Epp]*
     Maun kaun nijch met däm Kopp derjch 'ne Waunt gone. [R.]
     One cannot go through the wall with the head.
     Man kann nicht mit dem Kopf durch die Wand gehen.

762) Jnod jeiht ver Raicht. *[Epp]*
     Jnod jeit fer Raijcht. [Rempel]
     Mercy comes before justice.
     Gnade geht vor Recht.

763) Een goodet Jewesse es een saunftet Koppkjesse.
     A good conscience is a soft pillow.
     Ein gutes Gewissen ist ein sanftes Kopfkissen.

764) Daut traft dän Noagel opp'em Kopp.
     To hit the nail on the head.
     Das trifft den Nägel auf den Kopf treffen.

765) De Ama jeiht soo lang nom Borm, bott et braikt. *[Epp]*
     Dee Ama jeit soo lang n'om Borm, bott et braikt. [Rempel]
     The pail goes to the well so long, until it breaks.
     Der Eimer geht so lang zum Brunnen, bis es bricht.

766) Et es een fuulet Schop, daut daut Woll nich droage well. *[Epp]*
     Et es een fület Schop, daut daut Woll nijch droage well. [Rempel]

It is a lazy sheep, that does not want to carry the wool.
Es ist ein faules Schaf, das die Wolle nicht tragen will.

767) Opprechtigkjeit hällt aum länsten uut. *[Epp]*
   Opprejchtijchkjeit hällt aum länjsten üt. [Rempel]
   Honesty endures [holds out] the longest.
   Ehrlichkeit erhällt am längsten aus.

768) Jääjensautze traikt aun. *[Epp]*
   Jääjensautse traikt aun. [Rempel]
   Opposites attract.
   Gegensätze ziehen an.

769) Meed haft sikj oppjehonge.
   "Tired" hung itself.
   Ermüdung hat sich aufgehängt.
   * *With this saying, children were being told to "stop complaining about how tired you are, and go back to work."*

770) Woo maun sien Bad moakt, soo schlapt maun.
   How one makes his bed, so one sleeps.
   Wie man sein Bett ordnet, so schläft man.

771) He haft sien Hoat en de raichte Stääd. *[Epp]*
   Hee haft sien Hoat enn dee rajchte Städ. [Rempel]
   To have the heart in the right place.
   Das Herz auf dem rechtes Fleck haben.

772) De Jlekjlichste send rikj,
   oba de Rikje send nich emma jlekjlich. *[Epp]*
   Dee Jlekjlijchste send rikj,
   oba dee Rikje send nijch emma jlekjlijch. [Rempel]
   The luckiest are rich, but the rich are not always lucky.
   Die Glücklichsten sind reich, aber die Reichen sind nicht immer glücklich.

773) Weada tohle kjeen Zoll. *[Epp]*
   Weada tole kjeen Ssoll. [Rempel]
   Words pay no toll.
   Wörter zahlen kein Zoll.

Talk is cheap.

774) Metjedeelte Sorj moakt haulf Sorj.
Shared worry makes half worry.
Geteilte Sorge macht halb Sorge.

775) Jlekjlich es dee, dee vejat, waut nich mea too veändre es. *[Epp]*
Jlekjlijch es dee, dee fejat, waut nijch mea too fe'endre es. [R.]
Happy is the one who forgets what can not be changed any more.
Glücklich ist er, der vergisst, was nicht mehr zu verändern ist.

776) Jietz es de jratste Oarmoot. *[Epp]*
Jiets es dee jratste Oarmoot. [Rempel]
Stinginess is the greatest poverty.
Geiz ist der größte Armut.

777) Een Schwien woat emma dän Blott finje.
A pig will always find the mud.
Ein Schwein wird immer den Schlamm finden.
* *Low-down people will always gravitate toward what is crude.*

778) Du best je noch gaunz naut hinja de Oahre. *[Epp]*
Dü best je noch gaunss naut hinja dee Oare. [Rempel]
You are really still wet behind the ears.
Du bist je noch ganz nass hinter den Ohren.

779) Schoare brinje Jlekj.
Pottery shards bring luck.
Scherben bringen Glück.
* *Reportedly said when a plate or bowl was accidently broken. To make the
   "breaker" feel better?*

780) Ried sachta, goh wieda.
Ride slower, go farther.
Reit langsamer, geh weiter.
* *Patience gets you further in the long run. Also, a horse ridden rapidly will
   tire quickly.*

781) Goode Dinja motte jeeewt senne.
Good things must be practiced.
Gute Dinge müssen geübt sein.

149

782) Bäta riede aus jeräde woare.
Better to ride than to be ridden.
Besser reiten als geritten werden.

783) Verjedoone un nohbed<u>ocht</u>, haft noch vääl Sorj jebr<u>ocht</u>. *[Epp]*
Ferjedoone onn nobed<u>ocht</u>, haft noch fäl Sorj jebr<u>ocht</u>. [R.]
Done before and reconsidered, has already brought us much sorrow.
Vorgetan und nachbedacht, hat schon viel Leid gebracht.

784) Schlaichte Jesalschoft vedoawt goode Sitte. *[Epp]*
Schlajchte Jesalschoft fedoawt goode Sitte. [Rempel]
Bad company spoils good manners.
Schlechte Gesellschaft verdirbt gute Sitten.

Kjenne Se een Peat riede? [www.freeimages.co.uk]

785) Een goodet Peat brukt kjeene Pitsch. *[Epp]*
Een goodet Peat bruckt kjeene Pitsch. [Rempel]
A good horse needs no whip.
Ein gutes Pferd braucht keine Peitsche.

786) Uk en'e Aikj mott et rein senne. *[Epp]*
Uck enn'e Akj mott et rein senne. [Rempel]
Even in the corner, it must be clean.
Auch in der Eck' muss es sauber sein.
  * A job must be done completely, and to be called clean a thing must be totally
    clean.

787) Eia leahre 'ne Hahn nich. *[Epp]*
Eia leare eene Han nijch. [Rempel]
Eggs don't teach a hen.
Eier lernen eine Henne nicht.

788) Best du nich schekjlich, soo doo schekjlich! *[Epp]*
Best dü nijch schekjlijch, soo doo schekjlijch! [Rempel]
Are you not stylish, then act with class [properly].
Bist du nicht schicklich, so tu schicklich!

789) Daut Latzte, daut Baste. *[Epp]*
Daut Latste, daut Baste. [Rempel]
The last, the best.
Das Letzte, das Beste.

790) De Fada es kjraftja aus daut Schweat. *[Epp]*
Dee Fada es kjraftja aus daut Schweat. [Rempel]
The feather is more powerful than the sword.
Die Feder ist mächtiger als das Schwert.

791) Eascht Bloome, dan Bäare.
First flowers, then berries.
Erst Blumen, dann Beeren.
* Success or reward comes in its proper time, so we must be patient.

792) Toovääl es unjesund; haulf soo vääl es uk jenuag. *[Epp]*
Toofäl es onnjesunt; haulf soo fäl es uck jenüach. [Rempel]
Too much is unhealthy; half as much is also enough.
Zuviel ist ungesund; halbsoviel ist auch genug.

793) Je wieda em Woold, je mea Brennholt. *[Epp]*
Je wieda emm Woolt, je mea Brennhollt. [Rempel]
The further into the forest, the more firewood.
Je weiter in däm Wald, desto mehr Brennholz.
* The deeper the commitment, the greater the reward.

794) Waut vom Woage foll es waig. *[Epp]*
Waut fomm Woage foll es wajch. [Rempel]
What fell off the wagon is gone.

Was fiel ab dem Wagen ist gegangen.
* Don't focus on the dead past.

795) Fuulheit moakt 'ne denne Supp. *[Epp]*
Fülheit moakt eene denne Supp. [Rempel]
Laziness makes a thin soup.
Faulheit macht eine dünne Suppe.

796) Vetruue, oba uk bestädje. *[Epp]*
Fetrüe, oba uck bestädje. [Rempel]
Trust, but also verify.
Vertrauen, aber auch bestätigen.

797) Wua daut Jeld rädt, es de Woahrheit stomm. *[Epp]*
Wua daut Jelt rädt, es dee Woarheit stomm. [Rempel]
Where money speaks, the truth is mute.
Wo das Geld spricht, ist die Wahrheit stumm.

798) 'Ne Kjast es kjeen Peatenkoop;
Blinja moak doch de Uage op! *[Epp]*
'Ne Kjast es kjeen Peatennkoop;
Blinja, moak doch dee Üage op! [Rempel]
A wedding is no horse-purchase; blind one, open your eyes!
Eine Hochzeit ist kein Pferdeinkauf; Blinder, tu doch die Augen auf!

799) Kjeepe oda nich, oba maun kaun doch schachre. *[Epp]*
Kjeepe oda nijch; oba maun kaun doch schachre. [Rempel]
Buy or not; but one can still haggle.
Kaufen oder nicht; aber man kann doch schachern.

800) Waut nich es, kaun noch woare. *[Epp]*
Waut nijch es, kaun noch woare. [Rempel]
What is not can still become [real, true].
Was nicht ist, kann noch werden.

801) Twee weete mea aus eena.
Two know more than one.
Zwei wissen mehr als einer.

802) Schnied nich dän Aust wuarauf du settst. *[Epp]*
Schnied nijch dän Aust wuarauf dü settst. [Rempel]
Do not cut the bough where you are sitting.
Schneid nicht den Ast woauf du siztst.

803) Leah nich en Fesch too schwame. *[Epp]*
Lea nijch een Fesch too schwame. [Rempel]
Don't teach a fish to swim.
Lehr nicht einen Fisch zu schwimmen.

804) Vääl kjenne mea aus eena. *[Epp]*
Fäl kjenne mea aus eena. [Rempel]
Many are more able than one.
Viele können mehr als einer.

805) De Toon moakt de Musikj. *[Epp]*
Dee Toon moakt dee Müsikj. [Rempel]
The tone makes the music.
Der Ton macht die Musik.

806) Wua aule dautselwje denkje, doa woat nich vääl jedocht. *[Epp]*
Wua aule dautselwje denkje, doa woat nijch fäl jedocht. [Rempel]
Where all think the same thing, there will not be much thought.
Wo alles desselbe denken, da wird nicht viel gedacht.

807) Maun mott sien eajnet Huarn blose. *[Epp]*
Maun mott sien äjnet Huarn blose. [Rempel]
One must blow his own horn.
Mann muss sein eigenes Horn blasen.

808) Je hecha de Boarg, je deepa de Dol. *[Epp]*
Je hejcha dee Boajch, je deepa dee Dol. [Rempel]
The higher the mountain, the deeper the valley.
Je höher der Berg, desto tiefer das Tal.

809) Rostrije Aix, saunfte Hänj, koldet Huus. *[Epp]*
Rostrije Akjs, saunfte Henj, koldet Hüs. [Rempel]
Rusty axe, soft hands, cold house.
Rostige Axt, sanften Hände, kaltes Haus.

810) Aufschuub es en beesa Gaust. *[Epp]*
Aufschüb es een beesa Gaust. *[Rempel]*
 Delay is an evil guest.
Aufschub ist ein böser Gast.

811) Waut maun jearn deit, daut schient nich schwoa. *[Epp]*
Waut maun jearn deit, daut schient nijch schwoa. *[Rempel]*
What one likes to do, that does not seem difficult.
Was man gern tut, dass scheint nicht schwer.

812) Befrie dichtbi, oba goh wiet too stähle. *[Epp]*
Befrie dijchtbie, oba go wiet too stäle! *[Rempel]*
Marry nearby, but to steal go far [away]!
Heirat in der nähe, aber geh weit zum stehlen!

813) De Sans haft en Steen jeschloage. *[Epp]*
Dee Sans haft een Steen jeschloage. *[Rempel]*
The scythe has hit a stone.
 Die Sense hat einen Stein geschlagen.
 * *Said when the ongoing action has just "hit a snag."*

814) Oole Jesatze un niee Jemies send de baste. *[Epp]*
Oole Jesatsa onn nie Jemies send dee baste. *[Rempel]*
Old laws and new vegetables are the best.
Alte Gesetze und neue Gemüse sind die besten.

815) Ordninj mott senne.
There must be order [or tidiness].
Ordnung muss sein.
 * *Order and tidiness are a common passion among the Germanic peoples.*

816) Sposs mott senne. *[Epp]*
Spos mott senne. [Rempel]
[There] must be fun.
Spaß muss sein.

[Alt.] "Sposs mott senne," säd de Diewel, doa kjitteld he siene Grootmutta
met de Mestforkj. [Epp]
*"Spos mott senne," säd dee Diewel, doa kjitteld hee siene Grootmutta
met dee Mestforkj. [Rempel]*

" There must be fun," said the devil, as he tickled his grandmother with the pitchfork."
"Spaß muss sein," sagte der Teufel, da kitzelnte er seine Großmutter mit der Mistgabel.

817) Motte es 'ne hoate Nät.
Must is a hard nut.
Muss ist eine harte Nuß.

818) Aum Owend woare de Fuule pienig. *[Epp]*
Aum Owend woare dee Füle pienijch. [Rempel]
In the evenings the lazy become industrious.
Abends werden die Faulen fleißig.
* In other words, when it's time for recreation, the lazy have more energy..

819) Oole Jewahntheit saul maun nich bräakje. *[Epp]*
Oole Jewantheit saul maun nijch bräakje. [Rempel]
One should not break old customs.
Alte Gewohnheit soll man nicht brechen.

820) Gooda Rot es dia.
Good advice is dear.
Guter Rat ist teuer.

821) Jadanke send frie.
Thoughts are free.
Gedanken sind frei.

822) Kjeena kaun twee Hares bedeene. *[Epp]*
Kjeena kaun twee Haress bedeene. [Rempel]
No-one can serve two lords [masters].
Niemand kann zwei Herren dienen.

823) Maun kaun nich 'ne Notel en'e Stremp vestäakje. *[Epp]*
Maun kaun nijch 'ne Notel enn'e Stremp festäakje. [Rempel]
One cannot hide a needle in a sock.
Man kann nicht eine Nädel in eine Socke verstecken.

824) De Rikje habe de Medizien, Oarme de Jesundheit. *[Epp]*
Dee Rikje habe dee Meditsien, Oarme dee Jesuntheit. [Rempel]

The rich have medicine, the poor, health.
Reichen haben die Medizin, Arme, die Gesundheit.

825) Weete es Macht.
To know is power.
Wissen ist Macht.

826) Macht jeiht ver Raicht. *[Epp]*
Macht jeit fer Rajcht. [Rempel]
Power [might] goes before right.
Macht geht vor Recht.
   * Justice often takes a back seat to power.

827) Weete moakt Koppweehdoag. *[Epp]*
Weete moakt Koppweedoag. [Rempel]
To know makes headache.
Wissen macht Kopfweh.

828) Waut mi nich brennt, daut blos ekj nich. *[Epp]*
Waut mie nijch brennt, daut blos ekj nijch. [Rempel]
Something that doesn't burn me, I do not blow at.
'Was mich nicht brennt, das blas' ich nicht.
   * If it doesn't bother me, I leave it alone.

829) Onopprechtigkjeit schleiht sien eajna Har. *[Epp]*
Onnopprejchtijchkjeit schleit sien äjna Har. [Rempel]
Dishonesty strikes its own master [lord].
Unehrlichkeit schlägt seinen eignen Herrn.

830) Väasecht es bäta aus Hinjasecht. *[Epp]*
Fäasejcht es bäta aus Hinjasejcht. [Rempel]
Carefulness [foresight] is better than hindsight.
Vorsicht ist besser als Nachsicht.

831) Lot ons een reina Desch moake.
Let us make [a] clean table.
Lass uns einen reinen Tisch machen.
   * Let us make a clean start, and put the past behind us.

832) De Jeist es wellig, oba daut Fleesch es schwack. *[Epp]*
Dee Jeist es wellijch, oba daut Fleesch es schwack. [Rempel]
The spirit is willing, but the flesh is weak.
Der Geist ist willig, aber das Fleisch ist schwach.

833) Daut Blaut haft sikj jewonge.
The page has turned itself [ie. a new leaf].
Das Blatt hat sich gewendet.

834) Daut steiht opp een aundret Blaut. *[Epp]*
Daut steit opp een aundret Blaut. [Rempel]
That is found on a different page [subject].
Das steht auf einem anderen Blatt.

835) De Dolle un de Schwacke send sikj selfst toom Fiend. *[Epp]*
Dee Dolle onn dee Schwacke send sikj selfst toom Fient. [Rempel]
The angry ones and the weak ones are enemy to themselves.
Die Zornigen und die Schwachen sind sich selbst zum Feind.

836) Een Uag sitt foaken mea aus twee. *[Epp]*
Een Üag sitt foaken mea aus twee. [Rempel]
One eye often sees more than two.
Ein Auge sieht oft mehr als zwei.

837) Oarmet Sot, oarme Arnt. *[Epp]*
Oarmet Sot, oarme Arent. [Rempel]
Poor seed, poor harvest.
Armes Saat, arme Ernte.

838) Et es nich jieda Jääja, dee daut Huarn goot blost. *[Epp]*
Et es nijch jieda Jääja, dee daut Huarn goot blost. [Rempel]
It is not every hunter, who blows the horn well.
Es ist nicht jeder Jäger, der das Horn gut bläst.

839) De Woahrheit es hala aus de Sonn. *[Epp]*
Dee Woarheit es hala aus dee Sonn. [Rempel]
The truth is brighter than the sun.
Die Wahrheit ist heller als die Sonne.

840) Vääl Fadre moake een Bad. *[Epp]*
    Fäl Fadre moake een Bad. [Rempel]
    Many feathers make a bed.
    Viele Federn machen ein Bett.

841) Enj goot, aules goot.
    Good end, all's well.
    End gut, alles gut.

842) Däm Blinja halpt kjeene Brell.
    Glasses do not help the blind man.
    Den Blinden hilft keine Brille.

Ekj ha' foaken miene Brell veloare. [www.freeimages.co.uk]

843) Et wea een Schlag en't Wota. *[Epp]*
    Et wea een Schlach enn't Wota. [Rempel]
    It was a blow in the water.
    Es war ein Schlag ins Wasser.
    * *It was wasted energy; a pointless gesture.*

844) Jlikj aus 'ne Reaj von Klosses siene Kjeaj,
    Oba se haude mau eene. *[Epp]*
    Jlikj aus 'ne Räj fonn Klosses sieneKjäj,
    Oba see haude mau eene. [Rempel]
    Straight as a row of Klassen's cows,
    But they had only one.
    Gerade als eine Reihe, von Klassens Kühe,
    Aber sie hatten nur eine.
    * *Klassen is a common Russian-Mennonite surname. This is a humorous or ironic*
      way of saying that something is not straight.

845) Peeta P<u>anna</u>, Bexsetr<u>ana</u>, scheet em <u>Ama</u>. *[Epp]*
   Peeta P<u>anna</u>, Bekjsetr<u>ana</u>, scheet emm <u>Ama</u>. [Rempel]
   Peter Penner, trouser-ripper, shat in the bucket.
   Peter Penner, Hosentrenner, schiss im Eimer.
   * A children's nonsense rhyme that originated in Plautdietsch. The name Penner
      is common among Mennonites, and notice that the High German "Eimer" does
      not fit the rhyme-scheme as well.

846) Fresch aunjefonge es haulf jewonne.
   Fresh begun is half won.
   Frisch begonnen ist halb gewonnen.

847) Vääl H<u>änj</u> moake schwind een <u>Enj</u>. *[Epp]*
   Fäl H<u>enj</u> moake schwind een <u>Enj</u>. [Rempel]
   Many hands make a quick end.
   Viele Hände, schnelles Ende.

848) Wua kjeene Kloag es, es uk kjeen Rejchta. *[Epp]*
   Wua kjeene Kloag es, es uck kjeen Rejchta. [Rempel]
   Where no complaint is, is also no judge.
   Wo keine Klage ist, ist auch kein Richter.

849) En oolet Russlaund fruag wi nich noh Meed. *[Epp]*
   Enn oolet Russlaunt fruag wie nijch no Meed. [Rempel]
   In old Russia we didn't ask not about fatigue [ie. about being tired].
   In alt Russland fragten wir nicht nach Müde.
   * You don't ask, because you assume that you're always tired, as is everyone else.

850) Een Maun ohne 'ne Fruu es aus een Maun ohne Wintahoot. *[Epp]*
   Een Maun one 'ne Frü es aus een Maun met one Wintahoot. [R.]
   A man without a wife is like a man with no winter hat.
   Ein Mann ohne eine Frau ist wie ein Mann ohne Winterhut.

851) Et jefft kjeen Iebel ohne Goot. *[Epp]*
   Et jeft kjeen Iebel one Goot. [Rempel]
   There is no evil without good.
   Es gibt kein Übel ohne Gut.
   * Every negative thing brings with it some redeeming element or consequence.

852) Seehne es jleewe. *[Epp]*
    Seene es jleewe. [Rempel]
    To see is to beliewe.
    Sehen ist glauben.

853) Frindschoft seakjt Frindschoft. *[Epp]*
    Frintschoft sääkjt Frintschoft. [Rempel]
    Kin seeks kin.
    Verwandtschaft sucht Verwandtschaft.
    * Relatives stick together out of love and fellowship, and sometimes for survival.

854) Too ändre un too vebätre send twee unjascheedliche Sache. *[Epp]*
    Too endre onn too febätre send twee unjascheetlijche Sache. [R.]
    To change and to improve are two different things.
    Zu ändern und zu verbessern sind zwei unterschiedliche Sachen.

855) Schmockheit es vehältnismässig. *[Epp]*
    Schmockheit es feheltnissmässijch. [Rempel]
    Beauty is relative.
    Schönheit ist relativ.

856) Goode Woah lowe sikj selwst. *[Epp]*
    Goode Woa lowe sikj selwst. [Rempel]
    Good wares praise themselves.
    Gute Ware loben sich selbst.

857) De Wenj habe Uahre. *[Epp]*
    Dee Wenj habe Uare. [Rempel]
    The walls have ears.
    Die Wände haben Ohren.

858) Een gooda Schlenkjafoot fällt nich. *[Epp]*
    Een gooda Schlenkjafoot fällt nijch. [Rempel]
    A good "stumblebum" does not fall.
    Ein guter Schlenkerfuß fällt nicht.

859) Oaja kaun nich ohne 'ne stoakje Haund stohne. *[Epp]*
    Oaja kaun nijch one 'ne stoakje Haunt stone. [Rempel]
    Anger can not stand without a strong hand.
    Zorn kann nicht ohne eine starke Hand stehen.

860) Daut Hoat liggt nich. *[Epp]*
Daut Hoat liggt nijch. [Rempel]
The heart lies not.
Das Herz lügt nicht.

861) Se gauf ahm dän Korf. *[Epp]*
See jeef am dän Korf. [Rempel]
She gave him the basket.
Sie gab ihm den Korb.
* She turned down his proposal to get married. He was "dumped" or jilted.

862) Een Leahra es bäta aus twee Beakja. *[Epp]*
Een Leara es bäta aus twee Bäkja. [Rempel]
A teacher is better than two books.
Ein Lehrer ist besser als zwei Bücher.

863) De Dommajon rädt wan de kluaka Mensch stell es. *[Epp]*
Dee Dommajon rädt wan dee klüaka Mensch stell es. [Rempel]
The dunce speaks when the wise person is quiet.
Der Dummkopf spricht wann der kluger Mensch still ist.

864) Een Dokta un een Foarma [Bua] weete mea aus een Dokta auleen. *[E.]*
Een Dokta onn een Foarma weete mea aus een Dokta auleen. [Rempel]
A doctor and a farmer know more that a doctor alone.
Ein Arzt und ein Bauer wissen mehr als ein Arzt allein.

865) Se send nich aula jlikj, dee met däm Kjeisa riede. *[Epp]*
See send nijch aula jlikj, dee met däm Kjeisa riede. [Rempel]
They are not all equal, who ride with the emperor.
Sie sind nicht alle gleich, die mit dem Kaiser reiten.
* Appearences often obscure real power, or the lack of it.

866) Bäta em Blott too stohne, aus dichtbi de Troon too krupe. *[Epp]*
Bäta emm Blott too stone, aus dijchtbie dee Troon too krüpe. [R.]
Better to stand in the muck, than to crawl near the throne.
Besser im Schlamm zu stehen, als nahe dem Thron zu kriechen.

867) Een kjleenet Jeschenkj es bäta aus een grootet Vespräakjnis. *[Epp]*
Een kjleenet Jeschenkj es bäta aus een grootet Fespräakjnis. [Rempel]

A small present is better than a big promise.
Ein kleines Geschenk ist besser als ein großes Versprechen.
   * *Better to possess something tangible now than cherish the hope of wonderful, but vague, future rewards. This is the voice of conservative realism.*

868) Schekjlich es aus schekjlich deit. *[Epp]*
   Schekjlijch es aus schekjlijch deit. [Rempel]
   Proper is as proper does.
   Anständig ist wie anständig tut.

869) Wan du een gooda Frind hast, brukst du kjeen Speajel. *[Epp]*
   Wan dü een gooda Frint hast, brukst dü kjeen Späjel. [Rempel]
   If you have a good friend, you need no mirror.
   Wenn Sie einen guten Freund haben, brauchen Sie keinen Spiegel.

870) Dee, dee aum baste spält, jewennt. *[Epp]*
   Dee, dee aum baste spält, jewennt. [Rempel]
   He who plays best, wins.
   Der, der spielt beste, gewinnt.

871) Malasch un Baikjasch stähle nich, de Lied brinje noh ahn. *[Epp]*
   Malasch onn Bakjasch stäle nijch, dee Lied brinje no an. [Rempel]
   Millers and bakers steal not, the people bring to them.
   Miller und Bäcker stehlen nicht, die Leute bringen zu ihnen.

872) Wan de Ferscht wenscht een Aupel, nähme siene Kjnaichte dän Boom. *[Epp]*
   Wan dee Ferscht wenscht een Aupel, näme siene Kjnajchte dän Boom. [Rempel]
   When the prince wants an apple, his servants take the tree.
   Wenn der Prinz einen Apfel wünscht, nehmen seine Knechte den Baum.
   * *European nobles were often parasites and wastrels in the eyes of commoners.*

873) Schrie nich, ver du velatzt woascht. *[Epp]*
   Schrie nijch, fää dü felatst woascht. [Rempel]
   Do not cry out before you get hurt.
   Schrei nicht, bevor du verletzt wirst.

874) Een Schietstremp moakt tieen. *[Epp]*
Een Schietstremp moakt tian. [Rempel]
One coward makes ten.
Ein Feigling macht zehn.

875) 'Ne Schooh woat nich jieda Foot pausse. *[Epp]*
'Ne Schoo woat nijch jieda Foot pausse. [Rempel]
One shoe will not fit every foot.
Eine Schuh paßt nicht jeden Fuß.
* Each situation demands a unique response.

876) 'Ne Fruu hällt heemlich bloos waut se nich weet. *[Epp]*
'Ne Frü hält heemlijch blooss waut see nijch weet. [Rempel]
A woman keeps secret only what she does not know.
Eine Frau halt geheim nur was sie nicht weiß.

877) Nuscht weajt weinja aus een Vespräakje. *[Epp]*
Nuscht wäajt weinja aus een Fespräakje. [Rempel]
Nothing weighs less than a promise.
Nichts wiegt weniger als eine Versprechung.

878) Rach es een nieet Onraicht. *[Epp]*
Rach es een nieet Onnrajcht. [Rempel]
Revenge is a new wrong.
Rache ist ein neues Unrecht.

879) Vespräakjasch felle dän Buck nich. *[Epp]*
Fespräakjasch felle dän Buck nijch. [Rempel]
Promises do not fill the belly.
Versprecher füllen den Bauch nicht.

880) Oaja heat kjeen Rot.
Anger hears no advice.
Zorn hört keinen Rat.

881) Een schlaichta Aunfang mag een goodet Enj moake. *[Epp]*
Een schlajchta Aunfank mach een goodet Enj moake. [Rempel]
A bad start may make a good ending.
Ein schlechter Anfang könnte ein gutes Ende machen.

882) Von Äwafluss kjemmt Jlikjjeltigkjeit. *[Epp]*
Fonn Äwafluss kjemt Jlikjjeltijchkjeit. [Rempel]
From abundance comes indifference.
Von Überfluß kommt Gleichgültigkeit.

883) Bäta Neid aus Metlied. *[Epp]*
Bäta Neid aud Metliet. [Rempel]
Better envy than pity.
Besser Neid als Mitleid.
* Better to be in a position that others envy, than to be pitied.

884) Een jewoarnda Maun es haulf jeradt.
A warned man is half saved.
Ein gewarnter Mann ist halb gerettet.

885) Ondank es de Welt ääh Loohn. *[Epp]*
Onndank es dee Welt ää Loon. [Rempel]
Ingratitude is the world's reward.
Undankbarkeit ist die Belohnung der Welt.

886) Wua Macht raicht haft, es Jeraichtigkjeit nich Macht. *[Epp]*
Wua Macht rajcht haft, es Jeraijchtijchkjeit nijch Macht. [Rempel]
Where power is right, justice is not power.
Wo Macht hat recht, ist Gerechtigkeit nicht Macht.

887) Lot de Doodes ruhe. *[Epp]*
Lot dee Doodes rüe. [Rempel]
Let the dead rest.
Lass die Toten ruhen.

888) Jlekj jefft en browa Maun siene Haund. *[Epp]*
Jlekj jeft een browa Maun siene Haunt. [Rempel]
Fortune gives a bold man her hand.
Glück gibt einem kühnen Mann seine Hand.

889) Sat ahm bitte kjeen Fleaj em Uah. *[Epp]*
Sat am bitte kjeene Fläj emm Ua. [Rempel]
Please put no flea in his ear.
Setz ihm bitte keinen Floh im Ohr.
*Don't give him ideas or stir him up.

890) Waut dree weete, es bekaunt bi aule.
What three know, is known to all.
Was drei wissen, ist bekannt bei allen.

891) De Uage send de Seel äah Speajel. *[Epp]*
Dee Üage send dee Seel äa Späjel. [Rempel]
The eyes are the mirror of the soul.
Die Augen sind der Spiegel der Seele.
* People's true thoughts and feelings often show in their eyes.

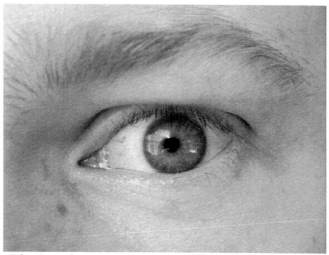
Disa Jung siene Uage send bleiw. [www.freeimages.co.uk]

892) Et es niemols bäta, en Kjäde aus frie to senne. *[Epp]*
Et es niemols bäta, enn Kjäde aus frie too senne. [Rempel]
It is never better to be in chains than to be free.
Es ist nie besser, in Ketten als frei zu sein.

893) Et es nich leicht, Mensch to senne. *[Epp]*
Et es nijch leijcht, Mensch too senne. [Rempel]
It is not easy, to be human.
Es ist nicht leicht, Mensch zu sein.

894) Bäta een kjleena Har aus een groota Kjnaicht. *[Epp]*
Bäta een kjleena Har aus een groota Kjnajcht. [Rempel]
Better a little lord than a great servant.
Lieber ein kleiner Herr als ein großer Knecht.

895) Jenuag es bäta aus een volla Sack. *[Epp]*
Jenüach es bäta aus een folla Sack. [Rempel]
Enough is better than a sackful.
Genug ist besser als ein voller Sack.

896) Et es goot dichtbi een Boot too schwame. *[Epp]*
Et es goot dijchtbie een Boot too schwame. [Rempel]
It is good to swim near a boat.
Es ist gut nahe einem Boot zu schwimmen.
* Make provisions for possible emergency.

897) Een kjleena Topp koakt boold. *[Epp]*
Een kjleena Topp koakt boolt. [Rempel]
A little pot boils soon.
Ein kleine Topf siedet bald.

898) Se schlope aula unja eene Dakj. *[Epp]*
See schlope aula unja eene Dakj. [Rempel]
They all sleep under one blanket.
Sie schlafen alle unter einer Decke.
* This means that they are as "thick as thieves," as close as confidants can be.

899) Pracha vääl, oba nemm waut aunjebode es. [Epp]
Pracha fäl, oba nemm waut aunjebode es. [Rempel]
Plead for a lot, but take, what is offered.
Bettel um viel, aber nimm was angeboten ist.

900) Bäta waut aus nuscht.
Better something than nothing.
Besser etwas als nichts.

901) Korte Hoare woare boold jeborscht. *[Epp]*
Korte Hoare woare boolt jeborscht. [Rempel]
Short hair will soon be brushed.
Kurzes Haar wird bald gebürstet.

902) Schwind huachstiee, schwinde Faul.
Rapid ascent, rapid fall.
Schneller Aufstieg, schneller Fall.
* Something like "easy come, easy go."

903) Heeflichkjeit es, waut Hett too Wauss es. *[Epp]*
Heeflijchkjeit es, waut Hett too Wauss es. *[Rempel]*
Politeness is, what heat is to wax.
Höflichkeit ist, was Hitze zu Wachs ist.

904) Heeflichkjeit kost't nuscht. *[Epp]*
Heeflijchkjeit kost't nuscht. *[Rempel]*
Politeness costs nothing.
Höflichkeit kostet nichts.

905) Aunfang es kjeen Meistastekj. *[Epp]*
Aunfank es kjeen Meistastekj. *[Rempel]*
Beginning is no masterpiece.
Anfang ist kein Meisterstück.

906) Pisch nich jääjen'em Wind;
Daut kaun em Jesecht spretze. *[Epp]*
Pisch nijch jääjen'em Wint;
Daut kaun emm Jesejcht spretse. *[Rempel]*
Don't piss against the wind;
That can spray in the face.
Piss nicht gegen dem Wind;
Das kann ins Gesicht spritzen.

907) Pisch nich een mien Borm. *[Epp]*
Pisch nijch enn mien Borm. *[Rempel]*
Don't piss in my well.
Piss nicht in meinen Brunnen.
* *Don't mess things up for me.*

908) Pomp oda du woascht vesupe. *[Epp]*
Pomp oda dü woascht fesüpe. *[Rempel]*
Pump or you will drown.
Pump oder du wirst vertrinken.

909) Soo aus eena d<u>eit</u>, soo et eenem <u>jeiht</u>. *[Epp]*
Soo aus eena deit, soo et eenem jeit. *[Rempel]*
[Loosely] As one does, so it goes for one.
So als man tut, so es man geht.

We shape our fate through our free will—actions have consequences.

PLAUTDIETSCH WORD INDEX

Plautdietsch	[English, Deutsch]	(by proverb number)

A

Aikj: 99, 234, 786   *[Corner, Eck]*
Aix: 629, 809   *[Axe, Axt]*
Äkj(e), -nät: 420   *[Oak, Eich]*
Älend: 439   *[Misery, Elend]*
Ama(sch): 419, 663, 765, 845   *[Bucket, Eimer]*
Angst: 235   *[Fear, Angst]*
Aprell: 417, 418   *[April]*
Arnt: 423, 837   *[Harvest, Ernte]*
Äsel(s): 111, 112, 113, 114, 215-20, 321, 758   *[Jackass, Esel]*
Äte: 71, 72   *[Food, Essen]*
Aufgonst: 446   *[Jealousy, Eifersucht]*
Aufschuub: 810   *[Delay, Aufschub]*
Aumt: 539   *[Office, Amt]*
Aunfang: 633, 634, 881, 905   *[Beginning, Anfang]*
Aunjreff: 299   *[Offense, Angriff]*
Auntwuat: 590, 649, 662   *[Answer, Antwort]*
Aupel: 26, 27, 28, 50, 139, 538, 872   *[Apple, Apfel]*
Aupetiet: 86   *[Appetite, Appetit]*
Aust: 802   *[Branch, Ast]*
Äwafluss: 504, 882   *[Abundance, Überfluß]*

B

Bäakja: 372   *[Brooks, Bäche]*
Bäa: 29,   *[Pear, Birne]*
Bäare: 30, 791   *[Berries, Beeren]*
Backe: 46, 67   *[Cheeks, Backen]*
Bad: 770, 840   *[Bed, Bett]*
Bädelsaikj: 66   *[Beggar-sacks, Bettelsäcke]*
Bassems: 747,   *[Brooms, Besen]*
Bea: 43   *[Beer, Bier]*
Been: 292, 454, 717   *[Legs, Beine]*
Bejia: 487   *[Greed, Habsucht]*
Bexe: 524   *[Pants, Hosen]*

Bie(e): 159, 268 *[Bee, Biene]*
Biedel: 366 *[Purse, Beutel]*
Biffel: 158 *[Buffalo, Büffel]*
Blaut / Bläda: 327, 398, 833, 834 *[Leaf, Blatt]*
Blinja: 798, 842 *[Blind person, Blinder]*
Bloom(e): 159, 380, 381, 791 *[Flower, Blume]*
Bloot: 700 *[Blood, Blut]*
Blott: 403, 777, 866 *[Mud, Schlamm]*
Boa(re): 135-39, 158, 474 *[Bear, Bär]*
Boarg / Boaj: 128, 428, 808 *[Mountain, Berg]*
Boat: 211 *[Beard, Bart]*
Bohne, -strooh: 325, 326 [Beans -straw, Bohnen -stroh]
Boll(es): 229, 272 *[Bull, Bulle]*
Boom / Beem: 206, 327, 331, 374-78, 394-99, 872 *[Tree, Baum]*
Boot: 896 *[Boat, Boot]*
Borm: 223, 663, 765, 907 *[Well, Brunnen]*
Borscht: 74 *[Borsht, Russian- Borshch]*
Botta: 569 *[Butter]*
Bräajen(s): 285 *[Brain, Gehirn]*
Brell: 842 *[Glasses, Brille]*
Brennholt: 793 *[Firewood, Brennholz]*
Brie: 55, 56, 57 *[Hash, Brei]*
Brigje: 754 *[Bridge, Brücke]*
Broot: 45, 46, 47, 51, 52, 54, 59, 67, 68, 69, 174, 179, 438, 475, 503, 519, 541, 615
[Bread, Brot]

Bruut: 267, 369 *[Bride, Braut]*
Bua(sch): 82, 97, 228, 864 *[Farmer, Bauer]*
Buak / Beakja: 271 *[Book, Buch]*
Buck: 64, 77, 492, 666, 710, 879 *[Belly, Bauch]*
Buddle: 695 *[Bottles, Flaschen]*
Bulkje: 54 *[Loaf, Laib]*
Busse: 529 *[Repentence, Reue]*

D

Däa(re): 350, 364, 439, 678 *[Door, Tür]*
Dack(je): 125, 133, 178 *[Roof, Dach]*
Dag: 16, 21, 385, 387, 689 *[Day, Tag]*
Dakj: 898 *[Blanket, Decke]*
Darscht: 35 *[Thirst, Durst]*
Deel: 296 *[Part, Teil]*
Desch: 507, 831 *[Table, Tisch]*
Diewel(s): 365, 509, 511, 531-36, 597, 620, 654, 816 *[Devil, Teufel]*
Dingj / Dinja: 290, 537, 742, 781 *[Thing, Dinge]*
Doagesoabeit: 744 *[Day's work, Tagesarbeit]*
Dokta: 542, 656, 657, 864 *[Doctor, Arzt]*
Dol: 808 *[Valley, Tal]*

Domm -ajons, -biedel, -heit, -kopp: 254, 320, 328, 331, 332, 863   *[Dumb, Dumm]*
Dood(es): 70, 90, 243, 405, 557, 649, 675, 749, 887   *[Death, Tod]*
Deef / Deew: 659, 667, 685, 686   *[Thief, Dieb]*
Dote: 460, 461   *[Deeds, Taten]*
Draikj: 109   *[Filth, Dreck]*
Drepp: 705   *[Drop, Tropf]*
Dulkje: 745   *[Imp, Teufelchen]*
Duuw(e): 109, 125, 126, 197, 603   *[Dove, Taube]*

E

Eah: 58, 242, 343, 494, 644, 748   *[Honor, Ehr]*
Ead: 330, 403, 414   *[Earth, Erd]*
Eadschocke: 307   *[Potatoes, Kartoffeln]*
Eelefaunt: 230   *[Elephant, Elefant]*
Eenheit: 293   *[Unity, Einheit]*
Eewung: 294   *[Practice, Übung]*
Eewigkjeit: 238   *[Eternity, Ewigkeit]*
Ei(a): 48, 49, 146, 222, 437   *[Egg, Ei]*
Ella: 255, 257, 260, 270, 281   *[Age, Alter]*
Ellre: 261, 269   *[Parents, Eltern]*
Enj(a): 36, 617, 633, 645, 703, 841, 847, 881   *[End, Ende]*
Enjel: 309, 687   *[Angel, Engel]*
Ente: 160   *[Ducks, Enten]*

F

Fada / Fadre: 790, 840   *[Feather, Feder]*
Fähla(sch): 311, 312   *[Mistake, Fehler]*
Fal: 133, 138   *[Pelt, Pelz]*
Faul: 902   *[Fall]*
Feld(a): 423, 507, 596, 684   *[Field, Feld]*
Fensta: 269   *[Window, Fenster]*
Fercht: 95, 639, 640   *[Fear, Furcht]*
Ferscht: 872   *[Prince, Fürst]*
Fesch(e): 106, 107, 108, 185, 201, 202, 803   *[Fish, Fisch]*
Fia: 249, 410-12, 442   *[Fire, Feuer]*
Fiend, -schoft: 600, 643, 644, 660, 835   *[Enemy, Feind]*
Finja(sch): 269   *[Finger]*
Fleaj(e): 87, 152, 153, 162, 175, 207, 230, 532, 889   *[Flea, Floh]*
Fleesch: 832   *[Flesh, Fleisch]*
Fliet: 611   *[Diligence, Fleiss]*
Fluss(e): 183, 373   *[River, Fluß]*
Foarma(sch): 35, 82, 97, 156, 228, 307, 409, 864   *[Farmer, Bauer]*
Foarmhund: 154   *[Farmdog, Bauernhund / Hofhund]*
Foot / Feet: 321, 875 [also 858]   *[Foot, Fuß]*
Forkj: 613, 630   *[Fork, Gabel]*
Foss: 96, 104, 158, 186, 187   *[Fox, Fuchs]*

Fräd: 596, 597, 682   *[Peace, Friede]*
Frädhoff: 657   *[Cemetery, Friedhof]*
Fräte: 78   *[Fodder, Fressen]*
Freid: 720   *[Joy, Freude]*
Frieheit: 223, 509   *[Freedom, Freiheit]*
Friesennigkjeit: 509   *[Liberality, Freisinnigkeit]*
Frint / Frind, -schoft: 310, 355, 371, 379, 408, 478, 660, 699, 754, 853, 869
                                                    [Friend, Freund]
Froage: 469, 662   *[Questions, Fragen]*
Frucht(e): 31, 375, 377, 394   *[Fruit, Frucht]*
Fruu(es): 302, 303, 334, 345, 418, 626, 635, 682, 850, 876   *[Woman, Frau]*
Fupp(e): 356, 366   *[Pocket, Hosentasche]*
Fuule: 818   *[Lazy people, Faulen]*
Fuulheit: 481   *[Laziness, Faulheit]*

G

Gaufel: 58   *[Fork, Gabel]*
Gauns / Jans: 104, 151, 160, 166, 167, 228   *[Goose, Gans]*
Gaunta: 167   *[Gander, Gänserich]*
Gaust / Jast: 21, 277, 680, 810   *[Guest, Gast]*
Glaus: 496   *[Glass, Glas]*
Glaushuus: 554   *[Glass-house, Glashaus]*
Gloowe: 543   *[Beliefs, Glaube]*
Goade: 422, 624   *[Garden, Garten]*
Goadna: 337, 624   *[Gardner, Gärtner]*
Gold: 342, 349, 350, 364, 584, 679   *[Gold]*
Goot: 851   *[Good, Gut]*
Goot(s): 12, 359, 547   *[Asset / Good thing, Gutes]*
Gott: 334, 343, 505-13, 516-18, 520-28, 535, 540-42, 598, 734   *[God, Gott]*
Gottesdeehnst: 515   *[Religious service, Gottesdienst]*
Grauss, -kje: 415, 523   *[Grass]*
Grootmutta: 816   *[Grandmother, Großmutter]*

H

Häärinkj: 323   *[Herring, Hering]*
Hahn: 103, 787   *[Hen, Henne]*
Hakj: 379   *[Hedge, Hecke]*
Hamd: 241, 356   *[Shirt, Hemd]*
Har(es): 527, 528, 572, 671, 746, 752, 822, 829, 894   *[Lord, Herr]*
Hauls: 391, 498   *[Neck, Hals]*
Haundlung: 338   *[Action, Tätigkeit]*
Haund / Hänj: 47, 125, 141, 200, 425, 433, 588, 620, 622, 727, 809, 847, 859, 888
                                                    [Hand]
Head: 679   *[Hearth, Herd]*
Heeflichkjeit: 731, 903, 904   *[Politeness, Höflichkeit]*
Hei: 23, 367, 613   *[Hay, Heu]*

Heilja: 548, 602 *[Saints, Heiligen]*
Hett: 903 *[Heat, Hitze]*
Himmel: 653 *[Heaven, Himmel]*
Hinjasecht: 830 *[Hindsight, Nachsicht]*
Hoa(re): 74, 281, 661, 901 *[Hair, Haar]*
Hoad: 130, 169, 224 *[Shepherd, Hirt]*
Hoat: 75, 251, 442, 514, 529, 666, 733, 771, 860 *[Heart, Herz]*
Hoawst: 38, 407 *[Autumn, Herbst]*
Hoftje(s): 165, 197 *[Hawk, Falken]*
Hohn(s): 96, 98, 99, 100, 101, 102, 154 *[Rooster, Huhn]*
Homa: 352 *[Hammer]*
Hommels: 450 *[Bumblebees, Hummels]*
Honnig: 135, 159, 268, 450 *[Honey, Honig]*
Hoofiesa: 192 *[Horseshoe, Hufeisen]*
Hoot: 576, 588, 755 *[Hat, Hut]*
Hopps: 57 *[Hops, Hopfen]*
Hos, -kjes: 90, 132, 134, 186, 523 *[Rabbit, Hase]*
Howa: 184 *[Oats, Hafer]*
Huarn: 807, 838 *[Horn]*
Hund / Hunj: 88, 89, 90, 134, 135, 136, 168-77, 179, 188, 203, 218, 223, 245, 276, 436, 732 *[Dog, Hund]*
Hunga: 34, 43, 51, 69, 482, 493 *[Hunger]*
Hupe: 534 *[Pile, Haufen]*
Huus: 344, 669, 671, 672, 674, 675, 677, 681-83, 809 *[House, Haus]*
Huut: 267 *[Hide, Haut]*

I

Iebel: 547, 851 *[Evil, Übel]*
Ies: 111, 112 *[Ice, Eis]*
Iesa: 471, 706 *[Iron, Eisen]*

J

Jääja: 838 *[Hunter, Jäger]*
Jääjensautze: 768 *[Opposites, Gegensätze]*
Jebäde: 42, 177, 360 *[Prayers, Gebete]*
Jeboot: 473 *[Commandment, Gebot]*
Jedaichtnis: 430 *[Remembrance, Gedächtnis]*
Jedocht / Jedanke: 339, 577, 722, 821 *[Thoughts, Gedanken]*
Jeduld: 285 *[Patience, Geduld]*
Jefoah: 357, 637, 664 *[Danger, Gefahr]*
Jeft: 159 *[Poison, Gift]*
Jehirn: 691 *[Brain, Gehirn]*
Jeist: 832 *[Spirit, Geist]*
Jeld: 3, 340, 343, 343, 347, 354, 355, 358, 360, 366, 367, 371, 439, 542, 609, 797 *[Money, Geld]*
Jemies: 814 *[Vegertables, Gemüse]*

Jeraichtigkjeit: 886   *[Justice, Gerechtigkeit]*
Jeräte: 614   *[Tools, Werkzeuge]*
Jesalschoft: 784   *[Company, Gesellschaft]*
Jesang: 427   *[Song, Gesang]*
Jesatz(e): 472, 636, 749, 814   *[Laws, Gesetze]*
Jeschekj: 333   *[Figure, Geschick]*
Jeschenkj: 361, 867   *[Gift, Geschenk]*
Jeschmack: 66   *[Taste, Geschmack]*
Jeschrie: 130   *[Scream, Geschrei]*
Jesecht: 85, 906   *[Face, Gesicht]*
Jesundheit: 86, 824   *[Health, Gesundheit]*
Jewääh: 600   *[Weapon, Waffe]*
Jewahntheit: 819   *[Customs, Gewohnheit]*
Jewesse: 763   *[Conscience, Gewissen]*
Jietz: 776   *[Stinginess, Geiz]*
Jinja: 482   *[Disciples, Jünger]*
Jlekj: 119, 332, 422, 435, 490, 496, 663, 740, 779, 888   *[Luck, Glück]*
Jlikjjeltigkjeit: 882   *[Indifference, Gleichgültigkeit]*
Jnod: 762   *[Mercy, Gnade]*
Joah(re): 271, 281, 407   *[Year, Jahr]*
Jugend: 257, 161-65, 270   *[Youth, Jugend]*
Jung(es); 524   *[Boy, Junge]*

K

Kameel: 204   *[Camel, Kamel]*
Karakta: 354   *[Character]*
Kaulf: 93   *[Calf, Kalb]*
Kaut(e): 116 thru 123, 205, 206, 225-27, 245   *[Cat, Katze]*
Kjäde: 892   *[Chains, Ketten]*
Kjantnis: 239   *[Knowledge: Kenntnis]*
Kjast: 429, 798   *[Wedding, Hochzeit]*
Kjätel: 100   *[Tractor, Traktor]*
Kjeenig: 673   *[King, König]*
Kjees: 46, 68   *[Cheese, Käse]*
Kjeisa: 672, 865   *[Emperor, Kaiser]*
Kjind / Kjinja, -tje, -spell: 241, 246, 249-51, 269, 274, 275, 279, 280, 308, 485, 506, 521, 735   *[Child, Kind]*
Kjoakj(e): 530, 602   *[Church, Kirche]*
Kjoakjemuus: 501   *[Churchmouse, Kirchenmaus]*
Kjoasche: 30, 575   *[Cherries, Kirschen]*
Kjnaicht, -e: 746, 872, 894   *[Servant, Knecht]*
Kjnee: 251   *[Knee, Knie]*
Kjneppel: 668, 697   *[Cudgel or Club, Knüppel]*
Kjrigg: 597   *[War, Krieg]*
Kloag: 848   *[Complaint, Klage]*
Kluakheit: 708   *[Wisdom, Klugheit]*

Knoaka(-es): 170, 177 *[Bones, Knocken]*
Koch(s, -asch): 34, 55, 650 *[Cooks, Köche]*
Kold: 148 [Cold, Kälte]
Kooh / Kjeaj: 156, 193, 231-33, 259, 543, 844 *[Cow, Kuh]*
Koohschiet: 756 *[Cowshit, Kuhscheiss]*
Kopeck: 341 *[a Russian coin]*
Kopp: 106, 292, 442, 569, 576, 580, 601, 755, 761, 764 *[Head, Kopf]*
Koppkjesse: 763 *[Pillow, Kopfkissen]*
Koppweehdoag: 827 *[Headache, Kopfschmerz]*
Korf: 79, 861 *[Basket, Korb]*
Korn: 38, 101, 115 *[Corn, Mais]*
Kos(e): 161, 210, 211, 337 *[Goat, Ziege]*
Kota(sch): 98, 124 *[Tomcat, Kater]*
Kranke: 542 *[Sick person, Kranker]*
Krankheit: 255 *[Sickness, Krankheit]*
Krauj(e); 149, 150, 603 *[Crow, Krähe]*
Krulkje: 745 *[little curl or lock, Löckchen]*
Kruut: 405 *[Weed, Kraut]*
Kuarn(kje): 33, 129 *[Kernel, Kernchen]*
Kwol: 559 *[Agony, Qual]*

L

Lääj(es): 453-55 *[Lie, Lüge]*
Läajna(sch): 336, 468 *[Liar, Lügner]*
Läpel: 56 *[Spoon, Löffel]*
Laum: 92 *[Lamb, Lamm]*
Laund: 141, 142, 406, 588, 589 *[Land]*
Laust: 757 *[Burden, Last]*
Läwe: 236-44, 246-48, 427, 557 *[Life, Leben]*
Leahra: 179, 320, 862 *[Teacher, Lehrer]*
Leet: 45 *[Song, Lied]*
Leew(e): 117, 196 *[Lion, Löwe]*
Leew [love]: 418, 424-26, 428-39, 441, 443-48 *[Love, Liebe]*
Leewoakje: 653 *[Larks, Lerken]*
Licht: 511 *[Light, Licht]*
Lied: 42, 300, 306, 486, 647, 655, 696, 760, 871 *[People, Leute]*
Lief: 61, 709 *[Body, Leib]*
Loohn / Leehna: 513, 616, 619, 885 *[Reward, Lohn or Belohnung]*
Low: 387 *[Praise, Lob]*

M

Mäa: 373, 406, 655 *[Sea, Meer]*
Mäakje(s): 381, 440 *[Girl, Mädchen]*
Macht: 825, 826, 886 *[Power, Macht]*
Mähle: 520 *[Mills, Mühlen]*
Mala(sch): 661, 871 *[Miller, Müller]*

Malkj: 153, 229, 231-33   *[Milk, Milch]*

Massa(sch): 303, 650   *[Knife, Messer]*

Mässigkjeit: 619   *[Idleness, Untätigkeit]*

Maun / Mana: 7, 291, 314-16, 334, 335, 337, 345, 346, 390, 449, 536, 549, 589, 635, 652, 709, 850, 884, 888   *[Man, Mann]*

Meddelmässigkjeit: 694   *[Moderation, Mässigkeit]*

Meed: 769, 849   *[Fatigue; Ermüdung]*

Meew(e): 141, 142   *[Seagull, Möwe]*

Medizien: 529, 824   *[Medicine, Medizien]*

Meista: 294, 605, 676   *[Master, Meister]*

Meistastekj: 905   *[Masterpiece, Meisterstück]*

Menniste: 732   *[Mennonites, Mennoniete]*

Mensch(e): 157, 163, 360, 513, 519, 646, 668, 697, 734, 741, 760, 863, 893
                                        [People, Menschen]

Mest: 102, 347, 380, 384   *[Manure, Mist]*

Mestforkj: 816   *[Manure-fork or pitschfork, Mistgabel]*

Metlied: 127, 883   *[Pity, Mitleid]*

Minuut: 22   *[Minute]*

Moag: 62, 75, 426   *[Stomach, Magen]*

Moakjt: 566   *[Market, Markt]*

Moht: 730   *[Measure, Maß]*

Moltiet: 623   *[Mealtime, Mahlzeit]*

Moot: 136, 527   *[Courage, Mut]*

Morje –stund: 342, 385, 413   *[Morning, Morgen]*

Musikj: 805   *[Music, Musik]*

Mutta: 274, 279, 280, 440   *[Mother, Mutter]*

Muul: 63, 91, 179, 342, 514, 589, 691   *[Mouth, Mund]*

Muus / Mies: 115-18, 129, 226, 683   *[Mouse, Maus]*

N

Näakjstaleew: 500   *[Charity, Nächstensliebe]*

Nacht: 227, 636   *[Night, Nacht]*

Nachtjeschwien: 744   *[Nightly misbehavior, Nachtschweinerei]*

Nachtigaul: 189   *[Nightingale, Nachtigall]*

Nast: 105, 277   *[Nest, Nast]*

Nat: 365   *[Net, Netz]*

Nät: 817   *[Nut, Nuß]*

Natua: 404   *[Nature, Natur]*

Näwel: 414   *[Fog, Nebel]*

Neid: 883   *[Envy, Neid]*

Noa(re): 14, 305, 306, 308-10, 318, 319, 334, 335, 427   *[Fool, Narr]*

Noagel: 764   *[Nail, Nägel]*

Noba(sch): 275, 481, 669, 720   *[Neighbor, Nachbar]*

Nohrecht: 717   *[News, Nachricht]*

Noot: 6, 59, 68, 471-76, 478, 500, 502-04, 522   *[Need, Not]*

Notel: 823   *[Needle, Nädel]*

Nuade: 148 *[North, Nord]*

O

Oabeit: 236, 604, 607-09, 615, 616, 618, 620, 623, 626, 627, 759 *[Work, Arbeit]*
Oah(re) also Uah(re): 362, 778 *[Ear, Ohr]*
Oaja: 24, 880 *[Anger, Zorn]*
Oarme: 484-86, 572, 667, 824 *[Poor one, Armer]*
Oarmoot: 479-82, 487, 488, 619, 776 *[Poverty, Armut]*
Odla: 87, 193 *[Eagle, Adler]*
Ondank: 885 *[Ingratitude, Undankbarkeit]*
Onjlekj: 489, 490, 497, 663 *[Misfortune, Unglück]*
Onkruut: 392 *[Weed, Unkraut]*
Onopprechtigkjeit: 829 *[Dishonesty, Unehrlichkeit]*
Onraicht: 486, 592, 878 *[Injustice, Unrecht]*
Onwada: 141 *[Bad weather, Unwetter]*
Ooste: 670 *[East, Ost]*
Opprechtigkjeit: 767 *[Honesty, Ehrlichkeit]*
Ordninj, -ung: 668, 696, 815 *[Order, Ordnung]*
Oss(e): 93, 128, 213 *[Ox, Ochs]*
Otboare: 190 *[Storks, Störcken]*
Owend: 413, 689, 818 *[Evening, Abend]*

P

Pacht: 665 *[Rent, Miete]*
Papia: 723 *[Paper, Papier]*
Peat / Pead: 162-64, 180-84, 192, 212-14, 220, 601, 785 *[Horse, Pferd]*
Peatenkoop: 798 *[Horse-purchase, Pferdeinkauf]*
Pelz: 188 *[Pelt, Pelz]*
Persoon: 284 *[Person]*
Pilja(sch): 548 *[Pilgrim, Pilger]*
Pilztje: 79, 80 *[Mushroom, Pilze]*
Pinktlichkjeit: 9, 731 *[Punctuality, Punktlichkeit]*
Pitsch: 785 *[Whip, Peitsche]*
Ploage: 35 *[Plagues, Plagen]*
Pluag: 621 *[Plough, Pflug]*
Pogg(e): 140, 189, 190 *[Frog, Frosch]*
Prachasack: 491 *[Beggarsack, Bettelsack]*
Pracht: 286 *[Pride, Hochmut]*
Prädja(sch), -sähns: 272, 546 *[Preacher, Prediger]*
Preisse: 692 *[Prussians, Preussen]*
Pries: 611 *[Price, Preis]*
Puat: 352 *[Gate, Tor]*

R

Rääjenwada: 107 *[Rainy weather, Regenwetter]*

Rääjle: 751 *[Rules, Regeln]*
Rach: 878 *[Revenge, Rache]*
Räd(e): 163, 582 *[Speech, Reden]*
Rädna: 468, 493 *[Speaker, Redner]*
Raicht: 762, 826 *[Right, Recht]*
Raubvääjel: 147 *[Birds of prey, Raubvögel]*
Raut: 234 *[Rat, Ratte]*
Reaj: 844 *[Row, Reihe]*
Reis: 607 *[Trip or journey, Reise]*
Rejchta: 455, 848 *[Judge, Richter]*
Rennlichkjeit: 248 *[Cleanliness, Reinlichkeit]*
Rigje: 754 *[Back, Rücken]*
Rikjdoom: 351, 721 *[Wealth, Reichtum]*
Rikje: 772, 824 *[Rich person, Reicher]*
Roos(e): 5, 382, 383 *[Rose]*
Rot: 1, 288, 302, 338, 508, 622, 758, 820 *[Advice, Rat]*
Ruak: 410, 411, 442 *[Smoke, Rauch]*
Rubel: 341 *[Russian currency]*
Ruh: 401, 579, 584 *[Peace, Ruh]*
Russlaund: 849 *[Russia, Russland]*

S

Sääj: 110 *[Sow, Sau]*
Sääjen: 516, 544, 598, 612 *[Blessings, Segen]*
Sähn(s): 423 *[Son, Sohn]*
Sach(e): 20, 448, 462, 487, 753, 854 *[Thing, Sache]*
Sack: 120, 123, 132, 133, 895 *[Sack]*
Sans: 813 *[Scythe, Sense]*
Saund: 200 *[Sand]*
Schaund: 494 *[Disgrace, Schande]*
Schaute: 152, 298 *[Shadows, Schatten]*
Scheffel: 269 *[Shovel, Schaufel]*
Schien: 115 *[Barn, Scheune]*
Schiet: 248 *[Shit, Scheiss]*
Schietstremp: 874 *[Coward, Feigling]*
Schildkjrät(e): 157, 198, 199 *[Turtle, Schildkröte]*
Schlachthuus: 110 *[Slaughterhouse, Schlachthaus]*
Schlag: 843 *[Blow, Schlag]*
Schmett: 740 *[Blacksmith. Schmied]*
Schlang: 126, 127 *[Snake, Schlange]*
Schlenj: 187 *[Snare, Schlinge]*
Schlenkjafoot: 858 *[Stumbler, Schlenkerfuß]*
Schmauntkaune: 701 *[Cream-cans, Sahnekrüge]*
Schmenje: 759 *[Tasting, Kosten]*
Schmockhiet: 855 *[Beauty, Schönheit]*
Schnee, -bala: 133, 453 *[Snow, Schnee]*

Schoare: 779   *[Shards, Scherben]*
Schode: 289, 553, 651   *[Tribulations, Schade]*
Schooh: 875   *[Shoe, Schuh]*
School: 476   *[School, Schule]*
Schop: 92, 131, 193, 208, 209, 766   *[Sheep, Schaf]*
Schopfleesch: 224   *[Sheepflesh or mutton, Hammel or Schaffleisch]*
Schrett / Schrääd: 71, 678   *[Step, Schritt]*
Schraikj: 99, 638   *[Terror, Schreck]*
Schrugg: 91   *[Nag, Gaul]*
Schuld(e): 221, 265, 357, 361, 642   *[Debt, Schuld]*
Schwalme: 155   *[Swallows, Schwalben]*
Schwaunz: 212   *[Tail, Schwanz]*
Schweat: 304, 790   *[Sword, Schwert]*
Schweet: 53   *[Sweat, Schweiß]*
Schwien: 109, 130, 195, 527, 777   *[Pig, Schwein]*
Schwon: 166   *[Swan, Schwan]*
Secht: 282   *[Sight, Sicht]*
Seel(e): 61, 365, 891   *[Soul, Seel]*
Selwa: 584   *[Silver, Silber]*
Senn: 282, 333, 582   *[Mind, Sinn]*
Sied(e); 290   *[Side, Seite]*
Sitte: 784   *[Manners, Sitten]*
Sittleah: 78   *[Morality, Moral]*
Sodel: 114, 214   *[Sadle, Sattel]*
Solt: 161   *[Salt, Salz]*
Sorj(e): 250, 348, 714, 720, 774, 783   *[Worry, Sorge]*
Somma: 434, 495   *[Summer, Sommer]*
Sompe: 140   *[Swamps, Sümpfe]*
Sonn: 416, 569, 839   *[Sun, Sonne]*
Soss: 167   *[Sauce, Soße]*
Sot: 2, 837   *[Seed, Saat]*
Spaikj: 109   *[Bacon, Speck]*
Spand(e): 159, 207   *[Spider, Spinne]*
Spauts(e): 125, 178   *[Sparrow, Spatz]*
Speajel: 284, 869, 891   *[Mirror, Spiegel]*
Spell: 435, 531, 607   *[Game, Spiel]*
Spoasaumkjeit, 344   *[Thrift, Sparsamkeit]*
Sposs: 816   *[Fun, Spaß]*
Spott: 553, 651   *[Mockery, Spotterei]*
Sprie: 716   *[Chaff, Spreu]*
Stääd: 44, 771   *[Place, Platz or Stätte]*
Stachel(s): 382, 283, 450, 563, 648   *[Thorn, Dorn]*
Stähl: 630   *[Handle, Stiel]*
Staul: 228   *[Barn, Scheune]*
Staum: 26   *[Stem, Stamm]*
Steen(a): 47, 554, 629, 705, 813   *[Stone, Stein]*

Stekj: 63   *[Piece, Stück]*
Stellness: 577   *[Silence, Schweigen]*
Stinkjkaut: 105   *[Skunk, Stinktier]*
Stolthiet: 331   *[Pride, Stolz]*
Storm: 401, 402   *[Storm, Sturm]*
Stremp: 823   *[Sock or Stocking, Socke or Strumpf]*
Strooh: 652   *[Straw, Stroh]*
Stroom: 372   *[Torrent, Strom]*
Student: 320   *[Student]*
Stund: 22   *[Hour, Stunde]*
Supp: 480, 795   *[Soup, Suppe]*

T

Tala: 100   *[Plate, Teller]*
Tähne: 170, 538, 541, 659, 661   *[Teeth, Zähne]*
Tausch(e): 370, 484   *[Purse, Tasche]*
Taxe: 665   *[Taxes, Steuern]*
Tiare: 235   *[Animals, Tiere]*
Tiet: 1-20, 606   *[Time, Zeit]*
Toofrädenheit: 721   *[Satisfaction, Zufriedenheit]*
Toon: 805   *[Tone, Ton]*
Topp: 73, 897   *[Pot, Topf]*
Trone: 606   *[Tears, Tränen]*
Troon: 866   *[Throne, Thron]*
Truarigkjeit: 366   *[Sadness, Traurigkeit]*
Tung: 303, 304, 316, 528, 580   *[Tongue, Zunge]*
Tuun: 441   *[Fence, Zaun]*
Twearm: 540   *[Thread, Gewinde]*
Tweiwel: 521   *[Doubt, Zweiffel]*

U

Uag(e): 4, 362, 363, 638, 639, 648, 798, 836, 891   *[Eye, Auge]*
Uah(re) also Oah(re): 77, 137, 316, 326, 457, 528, 701, 889   *[Ear, Ohr]*
Uasoak: 466, 500   *[Cause, Ursache]*
Utnohme: 751   *[Exceptions, Ausnahmen]*
Utwohl: 559   *[Choice, Wahl]*
Uul: 165, 191   *[Owl, Eule]*

V

Väälfros: 83   *[Glutton, Vielfrass]*
Väaschien: 726   *[Appearance, Anschein]*
Väasecht: 830   *[Carefulness, Vorsicht]*
Vejneaje: 608   *[Comfort, Vergnugen]*
Vemeaje: 369   *[Fortune, Vermögen]*
Vespräakje, -nis: 492, 867, 877, 879   *[Promises, Versprechungen]*

Vestaund: 433, 539, 712   *[Understanding, Verständnis]*
Veteidijung: 299   *[Defense, Verteidigung]*
Vetruue: 796   *[Trust, Vertrauen]*
Voagel / Väajel: 144, 145, 146, 148, 191, 200, 221, 222   *[Bird, Vogel]*
Voda: 423   *[Father, Vater]*
Vodalaund: 690   *[Fatherland, Vaterland]*

W

Wada: 102, 386, 418   *[Weather, Wetter]*
Waig / Wääj: 295, 300, 593, 729   *[Way, Weg]*
Wartel: 378   *[Root, Wurzel]*
Waste: 670   *[West, Westen]*
Waund / Wenj: 533, 761, 857   *[Wall, Wand]*
Waundavoagel: 143   *[Migratory bird, Wandervogel]*
Wausch: 642   *[Laundry, Wäsche]*
Wauss: 903   *[Wax, Wachs]*
Weat: 679   *[Worth, Wert]*
Weissheit: 712   *[Wisdom, Weisheit]*
Weit: 716   *[Wheat, Weizen]*
Welle: 295   *[Will]*
Welt: 52, 469, 668, 697, 885   *[World, Welt]*
Wensche: 240   *[Wishes, Wünsche]*
Wied: 444   *[Distance, Abstand or Entfernung]*
Wief: 427, 709   *[Wife, Weib]*
Wien: 62, 217, 305, 427, 695, 708   *[Wine, Wein]*
Wiendruwe: 84   *[Wine-grapes, Weintrauben]*
Wienglaus: 655   *[Wineglass, Weinglas]*
Wind: 399, 906   *[Wind]*
Winta: 99, 150, 155, 408, 409, 495   *[Winter]*
Wintahoot: 850   *[Winter hat, Winterhut]*
Wipp: 697   *[Whip, Peitsche]*
Woage: 794   *[Wagon, Wagen]*
Woah: 856   *[Wares, Waren]*
Woahrheit: 308, 451, 586, 797, 839   *[Truth, Wahrheit]*
Woakj(e): 464, 605, 617   *[Work, Werk]*
Woakjmaun, -mana: 604, 614, 627   *[Workman, Werkmann]*
Wolkj(e): 386, 416   *[Cloud, Wolke]*
Woll: 130, 766   *[Wool, Woll]*
Woold: 374, 393, 400, 793   *[Forest, Wald]*
Worscht: 36 thru 45, 52, 59   *[Sausage, Wurst]*
Wota: 107, 108, 180, 217, 221, 388, 389, 391, 498, 621, 700, 843   *[Water, Wasser]*
Wotaglaus: 402   *[Waterglass, Wasserglas]*
Wotalaicha: 654   *[Ponds, Teiche]*
Wuat / Wead: 235, 449, 450, 457-60, 464-66, 520, 733   *[Word, Wort]*
Wulf / Wilw: 94, 95, 208, 209   *[Wolf, Wulf]*

Wundadoda: 11   *[Wondrous deeds, Wundertaten]*
Wunde: 17, 465   *[Wounds, Wunden]*

Z
Ziel: 607   *[Goal, Ziel]*
Zoagel: 436   *[Tail, Schwanz]*
Zocka: 735   *[Sugar, Zucker]*
Zockamezpaun: 756   *[Sugar candy, Marzipan]*
Zoll: 773   *[Toll]*

SELECTED BIBLIOGRAPHY

Barbour, Stephen and Patrick Stevenson. <u>Variation in German</u> (New York: Cambridge University Press, 1990).

Becker, Rudolf K. <u>So Schabberten wir to Hüs</u> (Hamburg: Gerhard Rautenberg Verlag, 1975).

Dyck, Arnold. <u>Koop enn Bua en Dietschlaund</u> (Steinbach, Man: Derksen Printers, 1960).

------. <u>Koop enn Bua op Reise</u> (Steinbach, Man.: Derksen Printers, 1954).

------. <u>Onse Lied: Plautdietsche Jeschichte</u> (Uchte: Sonnentau Verlag, 2003).

Doerksen, Isaak and J.J. Neufeld, Ed Zacharias et al., trans. <u>De Bibel</u> (Winnipeg: Kindred Productions, 2003).

Dubrovin, M. <u>A Book of English and Russian Proverbs and Sayings</u> (Moscow: Prosvechceniye, 1993).

Epp, Reuben. <u>Dit un jant opp Plautdietsch- This and That in Mennonite Low German</u> (Hillsboro, KS: Readers Press, 1997).

------. <u>Spelling of Low German and Plautdietsch: towards an official Plautdietsch Orthography.</u> (Hillsboro, KS: Readers Press, 1996).

------. <u>Story of Low German and Plautdietsch: Tracing a language across the Globe</u> (Hillsboro, KS: Readers Press, 1993).

Fast, Peter. <u>Wie Räden en Läsen Plautdietsch</u> (Hillsboro, KS: Kindred Press, 1987) Children's primer, Plautdietsch only.

Goerzen, Jakob W. <u>Phonology of Plautdietsch</u> (manuscript, Bethel College Library, 1950).

Graf, A.E. <u>6000 Deutsche und Russische Sprichwörter</u> (Halle: M. Niemeyer, 1956).

Herrmann-Winter, Renate. <u>Kleines Plattdeutsches Wörterbuch für den Mecklenburgisch-</u>

Vorpommerschen Sprachraum (Neumünster: Wachholtz Verlag, 1985).

Himmelblau, Hannis. Junge, Junge!: Plattdeutsche Witze (Hamburg: Heinrich Bandholdt, 1909-10).

Huebert, Helmut. Hierschau: An Example of Russian Mennonite Life (Winnipeg: Springfield Publishers, 1986).

Klassen, Doreen Helen. Singing Mennonite: Low German Songs Among the Mennonites (Winnipeg: University of Manitoba Press, 1989).

Klassen, Heinrich. Mundart und Plautdietsche Jeschichte (Marburg: N.G. Elwert Verlag, 1993).

Kroeker, Evangeline. Schaule fon Frieyoa: Plautdietsch un English (Clovis, CA: E. Kroeker, 1988).

Lindow, Wolfgang, et al. Niederdeutsche Grammatik (Bremen: Schuster-Verlag, 1998).

Loewen, Jacob A. (Jash Leewe). Onze ieashte Missjounsreiz (Winnipeg: Mennonite Books, 1996).

Neufeld, Eldo. Dictionary of Plautdietsch Rhyming Words (München: Lincom Europa, 2002).

------. Dictionary of Plautdietsch Synonyms and Antonyms (München: Lincom Europa, 2003).

------. Plautdietsch Grammar: An aid to Speaking, Reading and Writing Netherlandic-Mennonite Plautdietsch (München: Lincom Europa, 2000).

------. Plautdietsch Humour (München: Lincom Europa, 2007).

------. Plautdietsch Verb Conjugation (München: Lincom Europa, 2000).

Neufeld, J.J., trans. Niehe Tastement: Plautdietsch (Hillsboro, KS: Kindred Press, 1987).

Panasenko, T.M. Ukrainian Proverbs and Sayings 2nd Edition (Kharkov: Folio, 2006).

Reimer, Al; Reimer, Anne and Thiessen, Jack, eds. Sackful of Plautdietsch: A Collection of Mennonite Low German Stories and Poems (Winnipeg: Hyperion Press, 1983).

Rempel, Herman. Kjenn jie noch Plautdietsch?: a Mennonite Low German Dictionary (Rosenort, MN: Prairie View Press, 1995).

Saint-Exupéry, Antoine de. Dee Tjliena Prinz. Jack Thiessen, trans. (Nidderau: Verlag

Michaela Naumann, 2002).

Sass, Johannes. Kleines Plattdeutsches Wörterbuch. (Neumünster: Wachholtz Verlag, 1997).

Skeat, Walter W. Early English Proverbs, chiefly of the thirteenth and fourteenth Centuries (Oxford: Clarendon, 1910).

Stellmacher, Dieter. Niederdeutsche Sprache: Eine Einführung (Bern: Germanische Lehrbuchsammlung Bd. 26, 1990).

Thiessen, Jack. Mennonite Low German Dictionary (Steinbach, MB: Hanover Steinbach Historical Society, 1999).

------. "A New Look at an Old Problem: Reasons for the Variations of the Dialects of the Old Colony and Molotschna Mennonites," Mennonite Quarterly Review 63, July 1988.